INTERESTING FACTS
FOR CURIOUS MINDS

1572 RANDOM BUT MIND-BLOWING FACTS ABOUT HISTORY, SCIENCE, POP CULTURE AND EVERYTHING IN BETWEEN

JORDAN MOORE

ISBN: 979-8-88768-002-6

CONTENTS

INTRODUCTION

If you're reading this, you're likely the kind of person who enjoys pondering some of the more obscure facts about our world. Maybe you've wondered how some seemingly unmedical things, such as alligator dung, became medical prescriptions.

Or perhaps you've wondered how marriage became the institution that it is today?

And maybe you've considered how crypto currency began, or how it works?

All of these questions, and many, many more are covered here in *Interesting Facts for Curious Minds: 1,572 Random, But Mind-Blowing, Facts About History, Science, Pop Culture, and Everything in Between.*

As the title indicates, this book takes you on a fun-filled odyssey through just about every nook and cranny of this planet, and far beyond, to bring you 1,572 factoids that will make you scratch your head and give you some fodder to impress your friends and family at your next gathering.

This book is divided into 63 chapters according to the subject matter, with 25 factoids per chapter. The book is written in a way that allows you to choose how it can be read. You can read it from cover to cover, or you can move back and forth, picking the chapters that interest you the most.

And as noted earlier, this book is a great conversation piece for parties and get-togethers. You can use *Interesting Facts* for friendly quizzes or just to break the ice, and it's also a good tool to learn a thing or two about your friends and family. Maybe you don't know the difference between an igneous and metamorphic rock, but by reading *Interesting Facts* with your best friend, you just learned that she's a geological whiz.

There are nearly unlimited options for what you can do with *Interesting Facts* and countless hours you'll spend having fun with this book. So, sit back and get ready to learn 1,572 of the most interesting - and sometimes strangest - facts that are known to humanity!

THE WILD WORLD OF MUSICAL INSTRUMENTS

○ The harmonica is the world's top-selling instrument, with about three million of the free-reed wind instruments sold globally each year. Its popularity is based on the fact that it is small, lightweight and affordable.

○ The kazoo is often a person's first musical instrument. An American original, the kazoo is likely derived from the eunuch flute, which is held horizontally while the kazoo is played vertically.

○ Spoons have been used as musical instruments for centuries. Former UB40 singer Duncan Campbell was once a registered spoon player with the United Kingdom's Musician's Union.

- A luthier is a person who makes a string instrument that has a neck and a sound box, which includes members of the violin family, guitars, banjos, and even the 42-string Pikasso guitar with four necks, two sound holes and 42 strings.

- Benjamin Franklin invented a lot of devices, but music lovers probably think his coolest invention was the glass harmonica (aka armonica). Invented by Franklin in 1761, the glass harmonica is a series of glass bowls arranged horizontally in graduated size (larger to smaller) that produce music through friction.

- Equine jaw bones make popular percussion instruments in some parts of Latin America. Known as the Quijada or Charrasca in Spanish, or simply the jawbone in English, the instrument was originally brought to the Americas by African slaves.

- With an estimated price of more than $20 million, the Messiah Stradivarius is the most expensive violin to ever exist. It was crafted in 1716 by Antonio Stradivari, a world-renowned maker of the best violins in the world. Stradivari created the Messiah during his golden period, and it stayed in his shop until he died in 1737. Violinists do not play with it as much, hence its relatively new condition.

- The Earth Harp is the longest stringed instrument in the world. Invented by William Close, the Earth Harp's strings extend up to 291.71 m (957 ft 0.6 in) and is installed in different locations that have optimal acoustics.

- The "world's smallest violin" is a real thing! Venezuelan luthier and violinist Baltazar Monaca performed Vivaldi's "Violin Concerto in A Minor" on a three-inch violin in 2014.

- *The Guinness World Book of Records* considers the Great Stalacpipe Organ in the Luray Caverns of Virginia to be the largest musical instrument in the world. The organ was first constructed by Leland W. Sprinkle in 1956 and covers 3.5 acres of the caverns.

- The harpsicord and piano may look like similar instruments, but they're actually in different instrument classes. The harpsicord functions by the strings being plucked, like other stringed instruments, while the piano works by hammers hitting the strings, making it a percussion instrument.

- If you ever watch the 1989 post-apocalyptic B-film, *Cyborg*, you'll notice many of the characters are named after musical instruments. There's the hero, Gibson Rickenbacker (Gibson guitars), the antagonist, Fender Tremolo (Fender guitars), and the cyborg, Pearl Prophet (Pearl drums).

- The popular instrument known as the Jew's harp is neither a harp nor associated with Jewish people. It originated in 3rd century BCE China and although it's plucked like a harp, it's played in the mouth.

- The Aztecs of Mexico loved music and human sacrifice, mixing the two in elaborate rituals. Death whistles were musical instruments carved out of different substances into the shape of human skulls that were used by priests during human sacrifice rituals.

- Before the record player/phonograph became affordable and popular in the 1930s, anyone who was anyone had a player piano, or pianola, in their home. Player pianos played programmed music on paper or metallic rolls.

- Clapperless cowbells are common in modern Latin music and can be heard in pop music from around the world by musicians who "want more cowbells." They are played by simply beating them with a drumstick.

- The theremin is a musical instrument that is played without physical contact. Invented by Russian Leon Theremin in 1919, the theremin is played by moving one's hands around and between two metal antennas.

- The sistrum was a hand-held percussion instrument that was popular in ancient Egyptian religious rituals. Music was made by simply shaking the sistrum, which rattled the metal rings that hung on it.

- A typical piano has over 120,000 parts, of which more than 10,000 of these move. Pianos also have more than 230 strings and 88 keys, making them one of the most complex instruments in the modern world.

- Late Nirvana's front man, Kurt Cobain's acoustic-electric 1959 martin D-18E sold for $6.1 million at an auction in 2020, making it the most expensive guitar ever sold.

- American engineer Robert Moog and his 1964 invention, the Moog synthesizer, changed popular music forever. The Moog synthesizer was groundbreaking because when it became available to the public in 1965, it became the world's first commercial synthesizer. It was used in the Beatle's album "Abbey Road" in 1969.

- If you're a fan of the film *Star Wars: A New Hope*, then you certainly remember the scene at the Mos Eisley cantina. The band actually had a name, Figrin D'An and the Modal Nodes, and the clarinet-looking instrument some of them were playing is known as a "kloo horn."

○ One of the oldest stringed instruments ever discovered is the "bull harp" or "bull-headed lyre." It was discovered in the ruins of the ancient Mesopotamian city of Ur (modern Iraq) and is believed to have been made sometime between 2,550 and 2,450 BCE.

○ Bucket drumming—simply playing the drums on one or more plastic buckets—has become popular in urban landscapes around the world. New Yorker Larry Wright is often credited with starting the modern music trend in 1990 when he was around 13.

○ You've probably heard a musical saw but didn't know it. A musical saw is simply a flexible handsaw that is held between the knees and played with a bow.

ECCENTRIC DICTATORS

○ In 1974, Spanish artist Salvador Dali gave to the Romanian dictator, Nicolae Ceauşescu, a scepter that he had made. The dictator treasured the gift, but most people at the time thought, and still do, that the clever artist was trolling the clueless autocrat.

○ Adolf Hitler was a vegetarian in his later years and near the end of his life ate only mashed potatoes and clear broth. The reasons for the dictator's dietary choices remain a mystery.

○ Soviet dictator Joseph Stalin was as brutal as they get, and also very paranoid. He was so paranoid that he had his scientists examine people's feces, believing he could determine their loyalty from it! During a visit by Mao ZeTong, he had his scientists examine Mao's feces to judge what mood he was in....

○ From 2005 to 2013 Mahmoud Ahmadinejad was president of Iran, but his first love was traffic. The tough-talking dictator actually earned a PhD in civil engineering and traffic transportation planning in 1997.

○ South Sudan's dictator, Salva Kiir Mayardit, was given a black Stetson by US President George W. Bush in 2006. Kiir Mayardit loved the gift so much that he bought a large collection so he's never without one.

○ Haitian dictator, François "Papa Doc" Duvalier (1907-1971) claimed to have cursed American President John F. Kennedy after he withdrew American support for him. Duvalier said he made a Voodoo doll of Kennedy and stuck it 2,222 times with a needle!

○ Over four short years, from 1975 to 1979, Pol Pot and the Khmer Rouge systematically exterminated up to 3 million people. The people of Cambodia had to live in fear, knowing that they might be the next ones dragged out to the Killing Fields. The chances of being chosen were indeed high – by the end of the massacre, the Khmer Rouge had wiped out nearly 25 percent of the population.

- Belarus strongman Alexander Lukashenko is known for his love of hockey, his fashion sense, and his belief in the right to bear arms. He had a custom-made golden pistol made for his son, who was five at the time.

- Kim Jong-Un of North Korea is reportedly a heavy drinker who has spent more than $30 million a year on booze. He is said to throw large parties but is also quite a heavy drinker.

- Mobutu Sese Seko Kuku Ngbendu Wa Za Banga did a lot of strange things when he ruled the Democratic Republic of the Congo (from 1971 to 1997 it was known as Zaire). One of the strangest was forcing the national TV news cast to depict him descending from the clouds in the opening credits.

- Cuban dictator Fidel Castro was a pragmatic leader. One of his best-known quotes is, "A revolution is not a bed of roses."

- Saddam Hussein was never afraid to tell people how he felt. In 1981, just after the Iran-Iraq War began, Hussein ordered a 1940 pamphlet that his uncle wrote, titled "Three Whom God Should Not Have Created: Persians, Jews, and Flies," to be republished and distributed in schools.

- Although a hardcore communist, North Korean dictator Kim Jong-Il (1941-2011) enjoyed the good life. For example, he once traveled by train across Russia and dined daily on lobster, which he ate with silver chopsticks.

- Joseph Stalin was actually born Ioseb Besarionis dze Jughashvili. When he moved from his native Georgia (the country, not the state) to Russia to embark on his revolutionary career, he changed it to the cooler-sounding Russian name, Joseph Stalin, which means "steel."

- In 1997, Saddam Hussein supposedly had a Quran written in his blood to celebrate his 60th birthday. The book is known as the *Blood Quran*.

- Before inheriting the presidency/dictatorship of Syria when his father died in 2000, Bashar al-Assad led a rather unassuming life. He was an ophthalmologist in London before his older brother Bassel died, making him the heir apparent to the presidency.

- Chinese dictator Mao Zedong never wanted his people to be too educated. He once said, "To read too many books is harmful."

- Idi Amin ruled Uganda with an iron fist from January 25, 1971, before being deposed on April 11, 1979. In that relatively short time, he did a lot of bizarre things, but one of the funniest was claiming to be the "uncrowned king of Scotland."

○ When "Papa Doc" Duvalier died in 1971, the rule was passed to his son, Jean-Claude Duvalier. The younger Duvalier was just as brutal as his dad, but he never quite got the same amount of respect, earning the nickname "Baby Doc."

○ Most World War II dictators had nicknames that are often translated into English as "leader." Hitler was Führer, Stalin was Vozhd, and Benito Mussolini of Italy was Duce.

○ Panama may be a small country, but Manuel Noriega was able to build a personal fortune of $300 million as its dictator from August 12, 1983, to December 20, 1989. He built the fortune through drug smuggling, CIA contracts, bribes, money laundering, and fraud.

○ Late Libyan dictator Muammar Gaddafi (1942-2011) was about as eccentric as you can get. His bodyguards were all females, he only stayed on the first floor of motels, and he often took his bulletproof Bedouin tent with him.

○ Stalin was said to routinely humiliate his subordinates and advisors. His successor as ruler of the Soviet Union, Nikita Khrushchev, even claimed that Stalin made him perform a traditional Ukrainian dance for a small gathering.

○ Francisco Macias Nguema managed to anger plenty of people in Equatorial Guinea with his outlandish ideas and policies from 1968 until he was removed in 1979. Perhaps the strangest thing he did was ban all boats and fishing in the country.

○ Idi Amin was no philosopher, but he was known to offer some good advice. He was quoted as saying, "You cannot run faster than a bullet."

FROM CROESUS TO CRYPTO

- Paper money was invented in China's Song Dynasty in the 11th century CE. Despite its widespread use at the time, no samples of Song paper money exist today.

- Although the US Federal Reserve was started by the government and is the country's tax-exempt central bank, its 12 bank branches have been cited as "independent, privately owned and locally controlled corporations" by the courts.

- The *deben* was the unit ancient Egyptians used for measuring weight. Although not a true currency, the deben was a standardized measure of precious metals.

- The inventor/developer of Bitcoin is believed to be a Japanese man named Satoshi Nakamoto. Many believe Nakamoto is actually a group of developers. So why has the anonymous Satoshi Nakamoto never come forward? Gyorfi believes the Bitcoin founder has remained in the shadows so that the digital currency is never connected to one person, to uphold it as a decentralized system in which no single person or group has control.

- The US dollar is the reserve currency of most nations and the official currency of several independent, non-US countries. Panama, Ecuador, El Salvador, the Marshall Islands, the Republic of Palau, and the Democratic Republic of Timor-Leste all use Uncle Sam's dollars.

- On June 28, 2021, El Salvador became the first nation in the world to make Bitcoin legal tender. Bitcoin is now accepted at Salvadoran retail stores and for taxes.

- As of March 2022, Elon Musk was the richest person in the world, worth more than $268 billion. Not bad for a nerd from South Africa!

- More than 20 countries use a dollar as their currency, including Canada, Australia, New Zealand, and the US. A thaler is one of the large silver coins minted in the states and territories of the Holy Roman Empire and the Habsburg monarchy during the Early Modern period. A thaler size silver coin has a diameter of about 40 mm and a weight of about 25 to 30 grams. It's believed that the use of the word began in Germany in the 1500s with coins known as the *thaler*.

○ You may find it hard to believe, but inflation was a problem in the Roman Empire. The debasement of the silver *denarius* coin, the Antonine plague (CE 165-175), and other factors led to an incredible inflation rate of 15,000% between CE 200 and 300.

○ When the "debt ceiling" was first created by the US Congress in 1917, it was $11.5 billion. It's now nearly $31 trillion!

○ King Croesus of Lydia (ruled ca. 560-540s BCE) is believed to have been the richest man in the world in his time. Croesus acquired his wealth by mining the silver-gold alloy known as electrum near the city of Sardis.

○ In November 2008, Zimbabwe's economy hit 6.5 sextillion percent inflation. The worst of the inflation occurred in November 2008 with a rate estimated at 79,600,000,000% per month, with the year-over-year inflation rate reaching an astounding 89.7 sextillion percent, leading to the abandonment of the currency.

○ In economics and finance, *fiat* is a term used to describe money that isn't backed by gold, silver, or other commodities. Fiat is a Latin term that means "let it be done."

○ Coin currency began in Lydia in the late 7th century BCE. The earliest coins were made of the gold-silver alloy, electrum.

○ The new shekel replaced Israel's previous currency, the Israeli shekel, in 1986. The term "shekel" is quite ancient, though, being used in the Near East in the 2nd millennium BCE as a measure of weight.

○ A troy ounce - which is used to weigh gold, silver, and other precious metals - measures 31.1 grams. A standard ounce weighs 28.3 grams.

○ A cryptocurrency is any decentralized, digital money/currency that uses cryptography to protect transactions and prevent fraud. Bitcoin became the world's first cryptocurrency in 2009, and now cryptocurrencies, as they're called, are a dime - or should I say, a Bitcoin - a dozen.

○ According to the Federal Deposit Insurance Corporation FDIC, one in 12 Americans is "unbanked," or they have no bank account. Note that home to 225 million adults without an account, China has the world's largest non-banking population, followed by India (190 million), Pakistan (100 million), and Indonesia (95 million)

○ Financial analyst and TV personality, Jim Cramer, proclaimed in February 2000 that there were ten stocks everyone should own. By 2009 all of those were either out of business or a fraction of their 2000 value.

○ The British pound, or pound sterling, is the world's oldest currency still in use. It was adopted more than 1,200 years ago and remains strong, as the fourth-most traded currency.

○ If you ever come across some gold or silver in your grandma's attic, you may have to have it metallurgically assayed. An *assay* is a chemical analysis of precious metal to determine its quality.

○ Midas was the ruler of the Anatolian Kingdom of Phrygia from about 738 to 696 BCE. Although he was wealthy, the idea that everything he touched turned to gold was added much later by the Roman poet Ovid (43 BCE-CE 17/18).

○ "Helicopter money" is a term used when central banks inject money directly into an economy to prevent a recession. This is achieved by funding programs, debt relief, or stimulus payments.

○ Most economists and historians believe the Amsterdam Stock Exchange was the first stock exchange in the world. Starting in 1602, it became part of the Euronext Exchange in 2000. Euronext N.V. is a pan-European bourse that offers various trading and post-trade services. Traded assets include regulated equities, exchange-traded funds, warrants and certificates, bonds, derivatives, commodities, foreign exchange as well as indices.

○ The US's gold bullion depository is held in a vault on a 42-acre complex next to the army base, Fort Knox, Kentucky. It houses more than 147.3 million troy ounces of gold.

SAY WHAT?

○ The Indo-European language family is the largest in the world, with 46% of the world speaking one of the languages. Most European languages, as well as Hindi, Iranian/Farsi, and others are in the family.

○ At 28 letters, the word antidisestablishmentarianism is thought by many to be the longest non-contrived and non-technical word in the English language.

○ A *polyglot* is a multilingual person. Many polyglots grow up in families or countries where multiple languages are common, while many are *autodidacts*, or self-taught.

○ Grammar, rhetoric, and logic were the three ancient arts of Greek/classical discourse. Grammar involves the mechanics of a language, including syntax, morphology, and phonology. Rhetoric is the art of effective or persuasive speaking or writing, especially the exploitation of figures of speech and other compositional techniques. Logic is a system or set of principles underlying the arrangements of elements in a computer or electronic device to perform a specified task.

○ British and American English spelling began diverging before 1776, but the big break came in 1828 when Noah Webster published the first edition of the *Webster's Dictionary*. After that, it was analyze, center, and labor for Americans.

○ Although the overwhelming majority of modern European languages are in the Indo-European family, Basque, or Euskara, is not. Basque is the primary language of about 750,000 Basque people in Spain and France.

○ Punctuation only gradually made its way into writing. Many believe the Moabite Stone, which is dated to 840 BCE Jordan, was the first text to use punctuation. It features points between words and vertical strokes to mark the end of sections that might be comparable to biblical verses.

○ If you really don't care about something, you "couldn't care less," not you "could care less." The latter implies you still have some caring to do!

○ English is a member of the Germanic branch of the Indo-European language family. Its linguistic ancestor was brought to Britain by the Angles, Saxons, and Jutes from continental Europe in the early 5th century CE.

○ Before 3,100 BCE, the first words were written in Egypt and Mesopotamia (Iraq). The earliest texts were simple words, but by 2,600 BCE, both areas were producing texts with complete sentences.

○ The Braille system of writing was invented by Frenchman Louis Braille in 1824. Braille lost his vision when he was a child of 3 years but developed the system of writing while he was a teen.

○ The Chinese languages, which include Mandarin and Cantonese, as well as Tibetan languages, are members of the Sino-Tibetan language family. More than 22% of the world speaks a Sino-Tibetan language.

○ A language revival is an attempt to stop the decline of a language or bring back an extinct one. Israel's support of Hebrew is the only example of a dead language successfully revived in the modern era.

○ A palindrome is a word that's spelt the same forward and backwards, like "madam" or "tot." You can also have a palindrome sentence like, "Sir, I'm Iris!"

○ The Gaelic language has no equivalent words for "yes" or "no." Instead, Gaelic speakers tend to say, "it is" or "it isn't."

○ A monoglot is a person who only knows or speaks only one language, while a bilingual person is fluent in a second language.

○ As much as people love *Star Trek*, grammar nerds are driven up the wall by the phrase, "To boldly go..." The word "boldly" splits the infinitive construction, making Captain Kirk sound cool but causing headaches to English teachers everywhere.

○ The Coptic language is directly descended from the ancient Egyptian language. Once spoken by millions of Egyptians as their primary language, it has been largely replaced by Arabic and is now heard primarily in Christian churches.

○ The serial comma, the comma before "and" in a series—i.e., Jim, Jill, and Becky - is also known as the Oxford comma. Surprisingly, the *University of Oxford Style Guide* advises against its use.

○ About 6% of the world speaks an Afro-Asiatic language, making it the fourth-most spoken language family. The Semitic branch of the family is the largest and includes Arabic, which is the first language of more than 350 million people.

○ English writer William Shakespeare modernized the English language. One way he did that was by adding new words to it, up to 1,700 by some estimates.

○ Most European languages use the Latin alphabet, which came from the Romans. The Romans got their alphabet from the Greeks who got the idea from the Phoenicians.

○ The *Oxford English Dictionary* adds about 4,000 new words to its pages every year. That means that a new word is added every hour and 40,000 new words every decade.

○ You can rearrange the letters of the word "silent" to spell "listen." This is called an *anagram*, which are much more common than you think.

○ Most countries have an official language, and several have more than one. The US, Argentina, Chile, Bosnia, Australia, New Zealand, and Japan are among the few that don't.

BEAUTY IS IN THE EYE
OF THE BEHOLDER

○ On average, an American woman will spend about $15,000 during her lifetime on beauty products. That includes about $3,770 on mascara, $2,000 on eye shadow, and $1,780 on lipstick.

○ Botox is actually a pretty toxic product. It's produced by the bacterium *Clostridium botulinum*, which can cause botulism. Botox works by causing temporary paralysis in the affected area.

○ The makeup worn by geisha women and kabuki actors in Japan is known as *Oshiro*. The word is translated into English as "white powder," because of its distinct, white appearance.

○ The modern word "tattoo" is derived from the Polynesian word *tatu*. Although many cultures throughout history have practiced tattooing, 18th-century British sailors brought the word into English when they witnessed Polynesian artists practicing their art.

○ The popular makeup company Make-Up Art Cosmetics (MAC) began with a more masculine touch. It was founded in Toronto, Ontario in March 1984 by Frank Toskan and Frank Angelo.

○ French company L'Oréal is the largest cosmetic firm in the world. The company started in 1909 as the Safe Hair Dye Company of France, quickly setting itself apart from the competition by employing chemists.

○ Women who wear makeup have been stigmatized at different points in history. Perhaps the most famous example is the Phoenician Queen Jezebel, who is described in The Bible's 2 Kings 9:30 as having "painted her face."

○ The US cosmetics industry is the largest in the world, but in second place is Japan's cosmetic industry. I guess all that *Oshiro* makeup can be expensive!

○ The practice of foot binding, where a girl or woman's feet were broken and tightly bound in order to change their shape and size, was popular in China from the 10th century until 1912. The deformed feet were referred to as "lotus feet" and were considered physically attractive.

- ○ Rhinoplasty is the technical term for a "nose job." The procedure is done by a maxillofacial surgeon.

- ○ A "Rubenesque" body type refers to one, usually a woman, who is curvy. The term is derived from the paintings of the Dutch painter, Peter Paul Rubens (1577-1640), who depicted curvy women as erotic and desirable.

- ○ In the 1700s powdered wigs were the fashion rage for men. People who wore them were among the "elites" in society. The first wigs were made from goat and horsehair, and because they were never properly washed, they smelled quite terrible and tended to attract lice. To combat the unfortunate odor and unwanted parasites, the wig-wearer would "powder" his wig.

- ○ The wars were very expensive exercises costing Great Britain the equivalent of £50 billion in today's dollar. The Duty on Hair Powder Act 1795 required that everyone wishing to use hair powder must visit a stamp office to enter their name and pay for an annual certificate costing one guinea (equivalent to £150 today). The trend ended in 1795.

- ○ Cosmetic testing on live animals has been completely banned in the European Union, Norway, Israel, Columbia, the United Kingdom, Australia, New Zealand, Taiwan, Guatemala, and India. Turkey, Brazil, and the US have partial bans.

- ○ In 1987, Venezuelan plastic surgeon Dr. Eduardo Krulig used the term *lipoinjection* for the first time. It involves putting fat into the body, usually the posterior, and is used for the now popular "Brazilian butt lift."

- ○ John Peter Mettauer is often credited with being the first American plastic surgeon. He performed the first cleft palate operation in 1827, thereby opening the door for nose jobs!

- ○ All brands of mascara are comprised of pigments, oils, and waxes. Many ingredients can be benign, such as beeswax, but others not so much, including titanium dioxide, oil of turpentine, and rayon microfibers.

- ○ The first breast augmentation surgery was done in 1962 on a 29-year-old Houston, Texas woman named Timmie Jean Lindsey. She went from a B to a C cup.

- Not wanting to be upstaged, American actress Liz Taylor refused to work with any woman wearing red lipstick. After all, red lipstick was one of Taylor's trademarks.

- The Chanel brand of perfume was started by Gabrielle Bonheur "Coco" Chanel in France during the 1920s. During World War II, Chanel collaborated with and spied for the Germans.

- The ancient Egyptians were among the first people to widely use cosmetics. Green malachite was used early in Egyptian history as an eye paint, but was later replaced by kohl, which was applied with a "kohl pencil or stick."

- Makeup icon Max Factor Senior's invention of the "beauty micrometer" has been largely forgotten. Factor built the contraption in 1938, which was supposed to identify parts of the face that needed more makeup, but it looked more like a medieval torture device.

- In the US, neon-colored nail polishes don't actually contain neon. The Food and Drug Administration (FDA) has banned the use of neon in cosmetics.

- Coco Chanel has also been credited with popularizing the suntan in the 1920s. Before that time tans were a sign of being working-class, but after Chanel, they became a symbol of leisure.

- Lead is a banned makeup ingredient in the US. Still, the FDA reports that 99% of the cosmetics still have some lead but at levels below ten parts per million.

- Although different types of nail polish have been used since ancient times, things changed in 1919. That was the year the first patent for nail polish was issued.

MASCOTS, CHEERLEADERS,
AND FANATICAL FANS

○ Professional cheerleader Krazy George Henderson led the first documented "wave" at an Oakland Athletics playoff game on October 15, 1981. It's since become a fan favorite activity everywhere.

○ Fan violence is not unique to the modern world. On Tuesday, January 13, 532 CE, chariot racing fan factions in Constantinople, known as the Greens and Blues, nearly brought down the Byzantine Empire in what is known as the Nika Riots.

○ Modern cheerleading began as an all-male venture in the US. Although cheerleading is now primarily female, it remains an American-centric activity.

○ During the early 1900s, the Chicago Cubs often used a live bear cub as a mascot. In 1908, though, they opted for a bear taxidermy mount.

○ Percy Abeysekera (born 1936) may be one of the most dedicated fans in the world. At 86-years-young, Percy has followed the Sri Lankan cricket team around the world and always waves the team's flag at matches.

○ It's believed that the first organized cheer at an American sporting event took place in 1884 at a Princeton University football game.

○ Johnny Campbell is often credited with being the world's first cheerleader. Campbell led a group of male University of Minnesota students in a cheer at a football game on November 2, 1898.

○ The National Basketball Association (NBA) Phoenix Suns' official team mascot is not a Sun, but a gorilla named "Go." Three different people have worn the gorilla suit.

○ Baseball is one American sport where cheerleaders are usually absent. Cheerleaders do play a big part in the Korean Baseball League's (KBO) fan experience, though.

- The San Diego Chicken is often credited with being the start of the American mascot craze. Ted Giannoulas first donned the outfit in 1974 and has been the only "official" Chicken since.

- Organized soccer/football hooligan clubs are known as "firms." It's believed that soccer hooliganism began in England in the late 1880s, but it wasn't until after World War II that the first firms formed.

- There are now dozens of professional and amateur cheer competitions around the world. Still, the National Collegiate Athletic Association (NCAA) doesn't recognize cheerleading as a sport.

- The 1980 Summer Olympics in Moscow, the Soviet Union were the first to have an official mascot. 'Misha the Bear' greeted Olympians and viewers from around the world in Moscow.

- In 1954, the Baltimore Colts became the first National Football League (NFL) team to have a cheerleading squad. They were part of the team's marching band and more closely resembled a high school or college cheer, squad.

- Major League Baseball's (MLB) Philadelphia Phillies' mascot is the "Phillie Phanatic." The green, flightless bird first entered the diamond during the 1978 season and is still the mascot.

- On April 30, 1993, a fanatical fan stabbed Yugoslavian tennis star Monica Seles during a match at the French Open. Although the injury was minor, she didn't compete for two years as a result.

- Since 1917, the official nickname and mascot of Yuma Highschool in Yuma, Arizona has been the "Criminals." The name comes from the original school being on the grounds of the old territorial prison.

- In 1972, the NFL's Dallas Cowboys Cheerleaders ditched the traditional look and went for sex appeal. They set a minimum age of 18 and traded skirts for hot pants!

- The Chicago Bulls won six NBA Championships in the 1990s. Fan violence and rioting took place following five of those wins: 1991, 1992, 1993, 1996, and 1997.

- Most hooligan firms also take nicknames. The English Premier League's West Ham United's firm is known as the "Inter-City Firm," while their main rival, Millwall's firm is called the "Bushwackers."

○ Three American presidents were cheerleaders in college. Franklin D. Roosevelt led cheers at Harvard, George W. Bush at Yale, and Dwight D. Eisenhower at West Point.

○ Until the late 1970s, Aniak, Alaska High School's mascots/nicknames were the Apostles for the boys' teams and Angels for the girls' teams. The students then voted to change the nicknames to the "Halfbreeds," which is what it remains.

○ The worst sports fan violence in African history took place on May 9, 2001, in Accra, Ghana. Supporters of the soccer clubs Accra Hearts of Oak clashed with Asante Kotoko, leaving over 127 dead.

○ Seven NFL teams don't have official cheerleading squads. The Green Bay Packers use a collegiate squad for home games that features more acrobatic maneuvers than dance.

○ Canadians love their hockey! Montreal Canadians fans rioted in 1986, 1993, 2008, and 2010 after their team won the Stanley Cup.

MAN'S BEST FRIEND

○ The once common dog name "Fido" came from the Romans. The name is derived from the Latin word, *fidelis*, which means "loyal."

○ An Australian cattle dog from Rochester, Victoria, Australia named Bluey is the longest-lived dog on record. Bluey lived 29 years, 160 days (June 7, 1910-November 14, 1939) before her owners had to euthanize her.

○ There's a common misconception that dogs don't sweat. Dogs have merocrine sweat glands, which are located on their paws.

○ Never feed your dog chocolate because it contains the potentially toxic alkaloid theobromine, which they can't metabolize. Small dogs can die from as little as 50 grams of chocolate.

- Each person's fingerprints are unique, but for dogs, it's their nose prints. The furless part of a dog's nose that contains the print is known as the *rhinarium*.

- Dogs are considered one of the most intelligent animals, but their degree of intelligence varies by breed. The border collie often tops most lists for intelligence, while beagles and basset hounds tend to be a bit on the slow side.

- The ancient Egyptians had two words for dog: *iu* and *chesum*. Egyptologists believe iu may have been onomatopoeic, referring to a dog's bark or sound, while chesum was a breed.

- Lassie was the most popular dog of the baby boomer generation. There were at least a dozen different Lassies, all males, that appeared in film and TV from the 1940s into the 1990s.

- An average dog's hearing is four times better than a human, but the part of their brain devoted to their sense of smell is about 40 times larger than ours!

- Domestic dogs are in the *Canidae* family, which includes wolves, foxes, and coyotes. They are in the genus *Canis* with wolves, jackals, and coyotes, but not foxes. Their Latin species name is *Canis familiaris* or *Canis Lupus familiaris*.

- Greyhound racing was once a popular sport throughout the English-speaking world and remains so outside of the US. There are only four active greyhound tracks left in the US, and two are set to close in 2022.

- Law enforcement around the world has used dogs to sniff out bombs and drugs, and in recent years they've also been trained to smell contraband cellphones in prisons.

- An adult dog has the intelligence of a human two-year-old. Dogs, though, can be trained easier than a kid and without the "terrible twos."

- Dogs can interbreed with other members of their genus, including jackals. The Sulimov dog is a jackal-dog hybrid that was first bred in the 1970s in Russia.

- Higgins was the name of the dog who played the lead role in the 1974 film, *Benji*. He got his acting start on the TV show *Petticoat Junction*. Although he died in 1975, like Lassie, several other dogs later played the role of Benji.

- The Labrador retriever has been in the top ten of the American Kennel Club's (AKC) most popular dog breeds for 31 years. It's known for its intelligence and friendly nature.

- You've probably noticed your sleeping dog twitching like he's having a dream. Well, scientists believe that dogs do dream in much the same was as humans.

- Although the ancient Egyptians didn't name most of their breeds, their texts and reliefs show they had basenjis, salukis, and greyhounds.

- The Dingo is Australia's wild dog. It is an ancient breed of domestic dog that was introduced to Australia, probably by Asian seafarers, about 4,000 years ago. Its origins have been traced back to early breeds of domestic dogs in south-east Asia

- When your dog kicks his hind leg after relieving himself, it isn't a weak attempt to cover the poo. No, Spot is merely marking his territory with the scent glands in his feet.

- A greyhound can run 35 mph for about seven miles, while a cheetah can run 70 mph for 30 seconds.

- Most American presidents have had pet dogs in the White House, but none caused a stir quite like Lyndon B. Johnson's beagles, Him and Her. He was photographed in 1964 pulling Him by his ears.

- On average, a dog can exert 15-20 pounds of pressure per square inch with its jaw. Some breeds, such as the pit bull, can exert up to 450 pounds per square inch.

- Fatal dog attacks are rare, with only 46 being recorded in the US in 2020. Pit bulls accounted for 72% of those fatalities.

- Newfoundlands are known to be great swimmers partly due to their webbed feet. On the other hand, basset hounds can't swim.

STRANGE INVENTIONS

○ The *cyclomer* was an amphibious bike that was invented in Paris in 1932. It had four air-filled floats to keep it up and was propelled by two fan blades that were attached to the spokes.

○ London designer Dominic Wilcox invented the finger-nose stylus in the late 2000s so he could use his iPhone in the bathtub. It's a long Cyrano de Bergerac looking nose that you strap to your head.

○ Valentin Vodev designed the roller buggy for parents on the go. It's a combination scooter-baby buggy, which makes me wonder if Vodev is a parent.

○ The Greek-Alexandrian scientist, Ctesibius (285–222 BCE), invented many devices. His most notable invention was a water-powered organ called the hydraulus.

○ Today there's an app for everything. There's even a "tampon app" that lets women know when it's time to switch things around.

○ Chester "Buck" Weimer's claim to fame is being the inventor of the world's first odor-proof underwear. The Colorado inventor received the patent for his fart-proof underwear in 1998.

○ The "hamster shredder" may sound awful, but it's actually pretty useful. It's a hamster cage with a paper shredder on top that's hamster powered!

○ Chinese inventor Lu Ban (ca. 507-444 BCE) has been credited for inventing the "wooden bird." It's not quite known what it was, but an ancient text stated it stayed in the air for three days, suggesting it was a kite.

○ The baby mop is a real thing. It's an infant onesie with mop strings attached to its front. I kid you not!

○ Ironing and coffee seem to go together, right? That was the idea behind the Ironius, the clothes iron-coffee mug combo, but it's yet to catch on.

- Kraft began selling sliced, processed cheese in 1950. But individually wrapped cheese slices were invented by Indiana engineer Arnold Nawrocki, who worked for the Clearfield Cheese Co, which released the product in 1956.

- In 1949, the "radio hat" started selling in American stores. Billed as the "Man-from-Mars Radio Hat," it was simply a portable radio built into a plastic safari helmet.

- The Japanese camera company Doryu produced the unique Doryu 2-16 from 1954 to 1956. This 16mm camera was special because it looked just like a semi-automatic pistol and even made a loud sound when the trigger was pulled, but this gun only shot pictures.

- Jaap Haumann invented the "anti-rape tampon" in South Africa in 2000 and was marketed in 2005. The device is inserted like a tampon, with a spring activating a blade on a potential rapist's jewels!

- The Roman engineer Vitruvius (c. 80-15 BCE) followed in Ctesibius's path in many ways. His most impressive invention was the early steam engine. His writings on anatomy were also the inspiration for Leonardo da Vinci's drawing, *Vitruvian Man*.

- Brit Harvey Adams is credited with inventing the "moustache cup" in the 1860s. The cup worked by having a ledge with a small opening that allowed liquids to pass without getting the whiskers wet.

- Snow protectors were invented in Canada in 1939 to protect against the harsh northern winters. They were simply plastic cones you put on over your face!

- Antikythera mechanism, is an ancient Greek mechanical device used to calculate and display information about astronomical phenomena. The remains of this ancient "computer," now on display in the National Archaeological Museum in Athens, were recovered in 1901 from the wreck of a trading ship that sank in the first half of the 1st century BCE near the island of Antikythera in the Mediterranean Sea. Its manufacture is currently dated to 100 BCE, give or take 30 years.

- The flask tie was invented for those who can't make it to happy hour. It looks like a regular corporate tie, but beneath the stripes is a pouch for your booze.

- There was actually a group shaving machine in the 1800s. It's no wonder why the device didn't make it in the era of straight razors!

- The Chinese inventor, Zhang Heng (CE 78-139), is credited with inventing the world's first seismoscope. His device could record the direction but not the time of an earthquake.

- The paternoster lift is a nonstop elevator with no doors, invented in 1868 in England. Due to the obvious safety concerns, they've been largely eliminated except for a few places in Europe.

- Charles Steinlauf invented the sewing machine bicycle in 1939 (aka The Goofybike). It was a pyramid-shaped contraption where two people peddled, the person in front steered, and a person in the middle used the sewing machine.

- Gunpowder was first invented in China in the 9th century CE, but it wasn't fully weaponized until it made its way to Europe in the 13th century. Europeans then brought muskets and cannons to East Asia in the 16th century.

- I'm not sure why, but there have been several patents awarded for "butt-kicking machines" in the US. The brothers Edmund and Ulysses De Moulin received a patent for their "initiating device" in 1908, which initiated a stream of similar inventions.

NO MAN'S LAND

- Tristan da Cunha is the most remote, inhabited archipelago in the world. The British Overseas Territory only has 250 permanent residents and is about 1,732 miles from Cape Town, South Africa, the closest major city.

- The legendary Easter Island is technically part of the nation of Chile, but it's a 2,300-mile trip from Santiago.

- If you go to the remote village of Katskhi in the Imereti region of the nation of Georgia, you'll find the Katskhi Pillar. It's a natural limestone formation with a 130 feet ladder that brings you to the ruins of a church on its peak.

- The national capital that's located the farthest from the next closest national capital is actually a tie between Wellington, New Zealand and Canberra, Australia. It just so happens that they are also each other's nearest national capitals at 1,445 miles.

- The Roanoke Colony, Virginia was too isolated from Britain. British attempts to colonize it in 1585 and 1587 ended in tragedy with all the 1587 colonists mysteriously disappearing.

- If you're interested in a truly remote vacation, contact White Desert Ltd. The British company offers five-star accommodations in Antarctica starting at $62,500 and ranging up to $98,500 per vacation.

- Tadmor Prison in Syria was once one of the world's most isolated prisons. Tadmor prison was located in Palmyra in the deserts of eastern Syria approximately 200 kilometers northeast of Damascus. Tadmor prison was known for harsh conditions, extensive human rights abuse, torture and summary executions.

- The Rub' al Khali or "Empty Quarter" covers over 250,970 square miles of the Arabian Peninsula. It is largely devoid of life and rarely crossed.

- After Mount Everest, Mount Aconcagua in Argentina is the most topographically isolated mountain in the world. The next highest peak after it is 10,265 miles away at Tirich Mir in Pakistan.

- North Sentinel Island in the Indian Ocean is home to the most isolated people in the world with 50-200 people. Since 1956, laws have prohibited outsiders from visiting the island.

- The world's most northern settlement with a population of at least 2,368 in 2019, is Longyearbyen, Norway. You can only get to the rest of Norway from there by airplane or boat.

- The monastery at Le Mont-Saint-Michel, France is located near a town, but its isolation is due to it being on a tidal island. Before a raised causeway was built in 1879, boats were the only way to get there at high tide.

- Wake Atoll is an American territory located 2,298 miles west of Honolulu and 1,991 miles southeast of Tokyo in the Pacific. Besides the United States Army and military, Wake Island is not home to any other humans except for a few contractors. The island's largest inhabitants are rats and hermit crabs. At one point, rats counted for two million of the island's population. No wonder the permanent population is...zero!

- A trade *embargo* is used by a group of nations to economically isolate one or more other nations. The term is Spanish, meaning "hindrance" or "obstruction."

- According to the Oxford Big Data Institute, Glasgow, Montana is located farther from a population center of 75,000 or more people than any town in the US lower 48.

- Iqaluit is the capital of Canada's Nunavut Territory with a population of approximately 7,740, but it has no highway connecting it to the rest of the country. You'll have to fly 1,300 miles to get from Iqaluit to the national capital of Ottawa.

- Ubar is a lost city mentioned in the Quran. In 1992, explorer Ranulph Fiennes led an expedition in the Empty Quarter to find Ubar, with mixed results.

- The Vikings established three settlements in Greenland in the late 10th century. Due to a combination of their isolation and global cooling, they were all gone by the early 16th century.

- The Sandhills is an approximately 20,000 square mile region of northcentral Nebraska that is hundreds of miles from a major city or even a four-lane highway.

- If you're flying from Rosario, Argentina to Xinghua, China, you're looking at the longest distance between two cities of 100,000 people or more at 12,425 miles.

○ Located on the very northern tip of Alaska is the lonely town of Barrow. Unless you're an ice road trucker, you can only get to this town via an hour and a half flight from Anchorage.

○ La Rinconada, Peru is the world's highest permanent settlement at 16,700 feet. It's also one of the most isolated, with the nearest airport being several hours' drive away.

○ North Korea is often called the "Hermit Kingdom" due to its political isolation. The term originally described Korea's Joseon Dynasty (1392-1897).

○ The Gurbantünggüt Desert in the Xinjiang region of northwest China is the farthest you can be on Earth from a coastline. The location 46°17'N 86°40'E in the desert is 1,644 miles from the ocean.

MARTIAL ARTS FROM AROUND THE WORLD

○ The term "martial arts" generally refers to any fighting style that has been standardized with a set of rules. The term "martial" is derived from the Roman god of war, Mars.

○ Modern boxing follows the "Marquis of Queensbury Rules," which was the code developed in England for the sport in 1867. Bare knuckles fights were eliminated in most places by the 1890s.

○ "Kung Fu" is a Cantonese Chinese term used to refer to many different styles of Chinese martial arts. The Mandarin term is Wushu, but they both can be translated into "martial art."

- The first documented use of the term "mixed martial arts" (MMA) was at the UFC 1 fighting event in 1993. The term is now used by dozens of leagues/promotions around the world.

- On December 3, 1810, Englishman Tom Cribb defeated former African American slave Tom Molineaux in what is considered the first world championship boxing match. It only took Cribb 35 rounds to win! But there was controversy over the decision and Cribb later had a rematch of 11 rounds where he defeated Molineaux.

- Action film star Jean-Claude Van Damme really does have an impressive martial arts background. He fought as a professional kick boxer and karate fighter, compiling an 18-1 record.

- Judo is a Japanese style of wrestling that was created by Jigoro Kano in 1882. Similar to Greco-Roman wrestling, Judo emphasizes throws, but ground grappling is also important.

- Olympic wrestling consists of two styles: Greco-Roman and freestyle. Both styles are based on the ancient Greek sport, but Greco-Roman competitors are not allowed to grab below their opponents' waists or use their legs for tripping.

- Pankration was the original mixed martial art. The Greeks introduced the sport, which combined wrestling and boxing, to the Olympic Games in 648 BCE. It was a no-holds-barred contest with few rules except for no eye-gouging or genital attacks.

- Taekwondo is a Korean martial art that emphasizes punches and high kicks. It combines the traditional Korean martial art of Taekkyeon with Japanese and Chinese styles.

- The Ultimate Fighting Championship (UFC) is the top MMA promotion in revenue, globally. In a distant second in revenue and market share is Bellator.

- The wrestling code practiced at the high school and collegiate levels in the US and some other countries is often called "folkstyle wrestling." Emphasis is placed on mat grappling.

- Sumo, which means "striking one another," is the national sport of Japan. Although many non-Japanese have competed as professional sumo wrestlers (rikishi), sumo is only practiced in Japan.

- The late Bruce Lee formed his own martial art he called "Jeet Kune Do." Jeet Kune Do combine Kung Fu and other Eastern arts with boxing and fencing.

○ Eastern martial arts are often collectively referred to as "Karate," but Karate is a specific fighting style that originated in Japan. Karate emphasizes strikes and began in the Ryukyu Kingdom (1429-1879).

○ UFC matches are fought in an eight-sided, caged ring known as "The Octagon." The standard octagon ring is 30 feet in diameter with a six-foot-high fence.

○ Capoeira is a Brazilian martial art that combines dance and acrobatics with a fighting style that emphasizes unorthodox kicks. Capoeira was invented by African slaves in the 1500s.

○ In addition to freestyle and Greco-Roman wrestling, boxing, fencing, taekwondo, judo, and karate are all Summer Olympic events. Karate made its debut at the Tokyo 2020 games.

○ Chuck Norris got his start in martial arts in the late 1950s when he was stationed in South Korea with the US Air Force. He was introduced to the Korean fighting style, Tang Soo Do, but eventually developed his own style, Chun Kuk Do.

○ The Russian martial art sambo was developed by the Soviet military in the 1920s. Sambo, which stands for samozashchita bez oruzhiya ("self-defense without weapons"), merged many different styles.

○ The Brazilian Gracie family are perhaps the most influential martial arts family today. The Gracies developed Brazilian jujitsu and Rorion Gracie was one of the founders of the UFC.

○ The 26th US President, Teddy Roosevelt, was a major advocate of martial arts. He trained in boxing, judo, and jujitsu.

○ *Gendai budo*, which means "modern budo," is the blanket term for all martial arts developed in Japan after 1869. Although aikido, karate, and judo all have ancient origins, they weren't fully developed until the modern era and are therefore gendai budo.

○ Brock Lesnar is known for his professional wrestling, but he also had a very "real" martial arts career. He was the NCAA heavyweight wrestling champion in 2000 and won the UFC heavyweight title in 2008.

○ The 2017 fight between boxer Floyd Mayweather and MMA fighter Connor McGregor was the biggest purse in history. Mayweather took home $275 million, while McGregor *only* earned $85 million.

POLITICS IS A DIRTY
AND FUNNY BUSINESS

○ John Stonehouse was a British Labour and Co-operative Party politician and cabinet minister under Prime Minister Harold Wilson who embezzled a bunch of money and faked his death in Miami, Florida in 1974. He was found to be very alive in Australia two weeks later, sent back to the UK, but only served three years in prison for fraud due to poor health.

○ On January 18, 1990, Washington D.C. mayor, Marion Barry, was arrested after smoking crack with a female informant in a motel room. Barry served six months in federal prison. He died later of a drug overdose.

○ The Russian word for blackmail is *kompromat*. During the Cold War, the KGB blackmailed so many Western politicians that kompromat made its way into the English language.

○ In 1824, a writer threatened to publish the memoirs of the Duke of Wellington's mistresses. The British duke's response was, "Publish and be damned."

○ Jack Ryan was the Republican candidate against Barack Obama for the open senate seat in Illinois in 2004 until it was revealed Ryan brought his wife to kinky sex clubs.

○ Former professional wrestler and full-time vampire, Jonathon (The Impaler) Sharkey, started the Vampires, Witches, and Pagans Party in 2005. They advocate for vampire political recognition.

○ Warren G. Harding is often regarded as the most corrupt US president in history. It's amazing because the 29th president only served two years before dying in office.

○ In 2014, Malaysian politician Bung Moktar Radin tweeted "Long Live Hitler" after Germany defeated Brazil 7-1 in a World Cup match. German officials didn't appreciate the support.

- Since the Watergate Scandal (1972-1974), many political scandals have been given the suffix "gate." For example - Troopergate, Russiagate, and Billygate.

- The Polish Beer Lovers' Party was established in 1990 in Warsaw, just as the Iron Curtain was coming down. It actually won 16 seats in Poland's Lower House before being dissolved in 1993.

- Nine American towns have elected dogs as mayors. Cat lovers can rest easy, though, the town of Talkeetna, Alaska elected an honorary feline mayor who served for 20 years from 1997 to 2017.

- When South Carolina Congressmen Mark Sanford went missing for a week in 2009, people were alarmed. When he finally surfaced, he said he was hiking the Appalachian Trail, but it was later revealed he was in Argentina with his mistress.

- Adolf Lu Hitler Rangsa Marak is a politician from India. When asked about the name, Marak said that his parents liked the name "and hence christened me Hitler."

- Former professional wrestler Jesse Ventura was elected as Minnesota's 38th governor in November 1998. He was the first American professional wrestler to hold such a high office.

- Tired of political corruption, 100,000 residents of Sao Paulo, Brazil voted for a female black rhinoceros named Cacareco for city council in 1958. Although she won more votes than the other candidates, election officials ruled Cacareco ineligible.

- US Congressman Hank Johnson said in a 2010 hearing on the territory of Guam: "My fear is that the whole island will become so overly populated that it will tip over and capsize." His office said it was a joke.

- American author Robert Anton Wilson formed the Guns and Dope Party. It was a bit of a joke Wilson had fun with during California's 2003 gubernatorial recall election.

- In addition to being involved in fraud, it was later made public that John Stonehouse had been spying for Czechoslovakia during the 1960s.

- Colorado US Senator Gary Hart looked set to win the 1988 Democratic presidential nomination when news of an extra-marital affair derailed his campaign. If only he ran *after* Clinton!

- Getting caught smoking crack on video isn't just an American thing. In 2013, Chris Farley lookalike and Toronto mayor, Rob Ford, got busted for smoking crack on tape, ending his reelection bid.

- Porngate is the name of one of the strangest scandals in Indian politics. The scandal involved two members of the Karnataka state cabinet watching porn on a smartphone when the legislature was in session in February 2012.

- American conspiracy theorist Lyndon La Rouche ran in every US presidential election from 1976 through 2004. Although a registered Democrat, he always ran as a third-party candidate.

- Democratic US Congressman Philemon Thomas Herbert shot and killed a waiter at a hotel in 1856. Herbert was acquitted of manslaughter, but the charges ruined his career.

- Empress Dowager Cixi of China (1861-1908) knew how to use blackmail as well as any man. Cixi tortured the concubines and servants of the Guangxu Emperor, her nephew, to use as kompromat against him.

- The late Japanese politician Mitsuo Matayoshi was the founder of the World Economic Community Party. His political platform consisted of fulfilling the Book of Revelation, as he claimed to be "The Only God Matayoshi Jesus Christ."

LITTLE KNOWN GAMBLING FACTS

○ Depend is a brand of undergarments for those with incontinence, but in 2014 they began targeting the casino crowd. The "Player's Advantage" line comes in a package prominently showing a royal flush.

○ Although dice games preceded the Romans, the Romans were the first people to bet on dice. The Romans called double 'ones' – 'snake's eyes' today - a 'dog throw.'

○ Blackjack is the most widely played casino game in the world. The game is derived from a French game called Vingt-Et-Un. It became known as blackjack in the US in 1899.

○ "Two-up" is a traditional Australian gambling game that involves throwing two coins in the air and guessing heads or tails. It's traditionally played on ANZAC Day (April 25).

○ *Parimutuel* refers to betting whereby all bets are put in a pool, and after the house takes its cut, the payoffs are calculated among the share of the total pool. Horse racing, dog racing, and jai alai are generally parimutuel bets.

○ In the US, each state government determines the legality and scope of gambling within its borders. Only Hawaii and Utah ban all gambling.

○ In the US, the term *sportsbook* refers to a place where bets can be placed on sports competitions. "Book" refers to the paper sheets gamblers often use to fill out their bets.

○ Jai alai is a popular Latin American sport with Basque origins, where betting is quite common. Florida has six frontons (jai alai venues) where you can place bets.

○ The tactic of "card counting" is not illegal in the US or UK, but if a casino knows or suspects someone is doing it, they'll be escorted from the property and usually blacklisted.

- A 2008 study revealed that American households earning less than $13,000 a year spend 9% of their income on lottery tickets.

- The royal flush (all one suit, ten through ace) is the best hand you can get in poker, but the odds of getting one are 649,739 to 1.

- A Canadian gambler named Brian Zembic won a $100,000 bet in 1996 that he'd get breast implants and keep them for a year. As of 2022, he still has the boobs!

- Nevada still holds the top spot as the US state with the most casinos, at 334. Oklahoma is number two with 134 casinos.

- Hawaii is listed on some websites as having two casinos. These two casinos are on cruise ships and although they leave Hawaii, gambling is only allowed in international waters.

- The Maya of Central America often made their prisoners play the deadly "ballgame." While the participants were playing for their lives, the nobles watching often placed bets.

- Gambling is illegal in most of China. The government does run two lotteries - the welfare lottery and the sports lottery - and casinos are still open in the once Western ruled cities of Hong Kong and Macau.

- The French card game baccarat was the favorite of the fictional character James Bond in the novels and early films. Baccarat was replaced by Texas hold'em as Bond's game in the 2006 film, *Casino Royal*.

- The New York based company, Sittman and Pitt, invented the first "gambling machine" in 1891. Players inserted a nickel, pulled a lever, and watched the five spinning drums. The drums and payouts were based on poker.

- Sports betting was once only legal in four American states, but since the Supreme Court ruled in 2018 that laws prohibiting it were unconstitutional, 28 states now allow sports betting.

- Sports gambling has been legal in the UK since 1960. Today, there are over 1,000 betting shops in London alone.

- Roulette is a French word that means "little wheel." Roulette is probably derived from the Italian game, biribi. In biribi, the players place bets on numbers that are on a board while the dealer draws numbers from a bag.

- The World Series of Poker (WSOP) began in 1970 when seven of the best poker players in the world met at the Horseshoe Casino in Las Vegas. Since that time, the WSOP has expanded to 101 events.

- Poker tournaments make sense, but did you know there are slot machine tournaments? In slot tournaments, competitors are given a set number of credits, then they simply start pulling the lever or pressing the buttons!

- FedEx founder Fred Smith once took the last $5,000 of his struggling company to Las Vegas and won $27,000. It was enough to pay the company's fuel bills.

- South Africa has the most casinos in Africa. The Rio Casino Resort in Klerksdorp, South Africa is the largest casino in Africa and the fifth largest in the world.

TRY SAYING POLYDACTYLY TWICE

- If you think you're a zombie, then there's a good chance you have Cotard's delusion. The mental disease makes the afflicted think they're dead, or undead. They often pass away due to a lack of food and water as they don't think they need to eat as they are already dead.

- Urticaria is a scientific term for a type of hive or skin rash. Most urticarias are caused by allergies.

- Fregoli delusion is a rare psychological disorder where those afflicted with it believe they keep seeing the same person in different places. For example, a Fregoli sufferer may see his father's face on people who are clearly not his father.

- People who experience panic attacks often think they're going to faint, but blood pressure raises during a panic attack, while fainting is usually caused by a sudden drop in blood pressure.

- Polydactyly is a condition where a person is born with extra toes or fingers. Former Mexican President Vicente Fox has polydactylism, with six toes on each foot.

- Necrotizing fasciitis is a bacterial infection that kills a body's skin and other soft tissues. It usually happens after a wound becomes infected and is then left untreated.

- A person who breaks out in hives from contact with water probably has aquagenic urticaria. A person with this affliction can drink water, but any external contact creates hives.

- Up to 20% of the American population may be allergic to the chemical nickel. This could be big considering that nickel is a major component in smartphones.

- The fear of long words is known as hippopotomonstrosesquipedaliophobia. I don't see how that long name helps those with this phobia, do you?

- Have you ever heard a gunshot as you were about to fall asleep? If so, you may have experienced exploding head syndrome (EHS).

- No pain no gain? Not if you suffer from congenital analgesia. Those with this rare genetic condition sense none or very little pain.

- If your urine has suddenly turned purple, you may have porphyria. Porphyria is a rare liver disorder that causes toxins called porphyrins to accumulate in the body.

- Progeria is a genetic disease that causes children to age seven times faster than normal. Children with progeria lose all their body fat and their hair, develop wrinkles, and usually die in their teens.

- From 1941 to 2009, there were 62 recorded cases of foreign accent syndrome. A person with this condition begins speaking in a foreign accent, usually after a traumatic head injury.

- If you've noticed that your girlfriend smells a little fishy, she may have trimethylaminuria. This happens when a person's body stores too much trimethylamine, causing a fishy odor.

○ Your constantly out of work brother-in-law may not be lazy. He could just be suffering from ergophobia or the fear of work!

○ About 1.3% of the population will experience pityriasis rosea at some point in their lives. It creates a rash over the torso, arms, and legs that last for up to three months. The causes of herpes related viruses are unknown.

○ Alaskans, Canadians, Russians, and Minnesotans may love winter, but for some it's deadly. People with cold urticaria can die if they are exposed to cold air for too long.

○ In rare cases, insomnia can be fatal. Fatal familial insomnia begins as a normal case of insomnia but quickly progresses to dementia and then death.

○ If you feel the urge to eat dirt, paint, or even feces, then you may have pica. Pica is the urge to eat uneatable things and although rare overall, 28-68% of all pregnant women experience it.

○ Noma is a rare infection of the mouth and face that's found primarily in the developing world. It's caused by poor sanitation, hygiene, and diet.

○ The next time you think about putting glitter on before a date, make sure he or she isn't allergic to mica. Most glitter is made from mica, which is also an allergen to some people.

○ Men and women can both be afflicted with persistent genital arousal disorder (PGAD). As the name indicates, those with the disorder are aroused physically for long periods of time, which can be an embarrassing problem for men.

○ Many people have found they're ironically allergic to allergy medication, although most scientists believe it's actually the dyes and additives in the medications that cause reactions.

○ It's believed the medieval Persian ruler Majd al-Dawla (ruled CE 997-1029) suffered from clinical lycanthropy. For a time, the ruler believed he was a cow.

THE SEARCH FOR GOD ENDS IN
SOME INTERESTING PLACES

○ From 1994 until May 2016, Wat Pha Luang Ta Bua Yanasampanno, better known as the "Tiger Temple," served as a Buddhist temple and tiger sanctuary in western Thailand. The authorities closed the temple for animal abuse.

○ The Church of Jesus Christ of Latter-Day Saints (Mormons) has thousands of churches around the world, but only 170 temples. Temples are reserved for special occasions.

○ The Karnak Temple in Luxor, Egypt is the largest religious complex in the world. It covers 247 acres of ground.

○ The Cathedral Basilica of St. Augustine in St. Augustine, Florida is the oldest continuous church congregation in the continental US. It was established by the Spanish on September 8, 1565.

○ Ziggurats were ancient Mesopotamian temple complexes that were built from about 3,000 to 550 BCE. They also served as scribal schools and astronomical observatories.

○ Work on the Parthenon in Athens, which was dedicated to the goddess Athena, began in 447 BCE and was completed in 432 BCE.

○ St. Peter's Basilica in Vatican City is ranked as the largest Christian church or cathedral in the world. Number two is The Basilica of Our Lady Aparecida in Aparecida, Brazil.

○ Zoroastrians believe that fire is sacred, so every one of their temples has a sacred fire that's continually kept. There are 167 Zoroastrian fire temples in the world.

○ Egyptian pyramids and Mesoamerican/Mexican pyramids may look similar, but they had different functions. Egyptian pyramids were tombs while those in Mexico were temples.

- Mount Fuji is the highest mountain in Japan and one of the holiest sites in the country. The Shinto and Buddhist religions both regard the mountain as holy.

- If you don't like rodents, stay away from the Karni Mata Temple in northwest India. Rats are sacred in this Hindu temple, with more than 25,000 roaming freely in it.

- The First Judaic Temple in Jerusalem was built during the rule of King Solomon around 957 BCE. It was destroyed by the Neo-Babylonians in 587/586 BCE.

- The Church of Saints Sergius and Bacchus is one of the holiest sites to Coptic Christians. The church was built in the 4th century at the site where the Holy Family is believed to have rested.

- The two largest mosques in the world are those in Mecca and Medina respectively, but the third-largest mosque in the world is the Grand Jamia Mosque in Karachi, Pakistan.

- The Batu Caves in Malaysia are a network of caves in a limestone mountain that is dedicated to the Hindu god Kartikeya/Murugan. The caves first became a holy site in the late 1800s.

- The Karnak Temple was primarily dedicated to the gods Amun-Re, Mut, and Montu, although smaller temples within the complex were dedicated to the gods Ptah and Khons.

- *The Guinness World Records* lists the world's smallest church as the Santa Isabel de Hungria in Benalmadena, Spain. It's listed at just under six square feet.

- Lalibela, Ethiopia is home to 11 rock-cut monolithic churches that were built from the late 12th to the early 13th centuries CE. The most famous is Bete Giyorgis/St. George, which is the shape of a cross.

- The largest pre-Columbian religious complex north of Mexico is the Cahokia Mounds in Illinois. The site existed from about 1050 to 1350 CE and covered six square miles.

- Scholars debate if the ancient Germanic peoples, including the Vikings, had physical temples. Some textual evidence suggests they did, but the archaeological evidence is lacking.

- The Temple of Confucius in Qufu, China is the largest Confucian temple in East Asia. The site is the former home of Confucius, who lived from about 551 to 479 BCE.

○ A reliquary is a small shrine that houses a relic. Reliquaries are usually located within the confines of a church, mosque, or temple, depending on the religion.

○ The Temppeliaukio Church in Helsinki, Finland is a unique site because it was built into solid rock. The Lutheran church was designed by brothers Timo and Tuomo Suomalainen, opening for services in 1969.

○ The Ziggurat of Ur was built by the Third Dynasty of Ur king, Ur-Nammu (2,112-2,095 BCE). The base measures approximately 190 by 130 feet, but only two of the probably three levels still exist.

○ The Hagia Sophia in Constantinople/Istanbul was originally built in the 6th century CE as a Christian cathedral, became a mosque after the Ottoman conquest in 1453, and was converted into a museum in 1935. But the government is now proceeding with returning it to a living mosque again.

GAMES, GEEKS, AND GADGETS

○ The first pocket calculators hit the market in Japan in 1970. The first American-made pocket-sized calculator was the Bowmar 901B. It sold for $240 a unit!

○ Before streaming there were DVDs, and before DVDs, there were video cassette recorder (VCR) tapes. But VCRs were challenged by Sony Betamax recorders and tapes until the former won the market share by the mid-1980s.

○ Microsoft founder Bill Gates scored 1590 out of 1600 on the SAT. It got him into Harvard, but he dropped out after two years to do "other things."

○ The predecessors to modern pinball machines can be traced back to the 1600s. The first coin-operated pinball machines began being placed in American bars and drugstores in the 1930s.

○ The 1980 arcade game, *Pac-Man*, originally came out in Japan as *Puck Man*. The name was changed when it was realized how vandals could have fun with the work "Puck."

○ The earliest version of the internet was the Advanced Research Projects Agency Network (ARPANET). It was started in 1969 as a special project of the Advanced Research Projects Agency Network (ARPA) of the US Defense Department.

○ *Starcade* was a gameshow that was broadcast on the TBS network in the US from 1982 to 1983. It featured contestants, usually teenagers, playing current arcade games against each other for prizes.

○ The video game *Spacewar!* Was developed in 1962 by programmer Steve Russell. It's important because it was the first video game available for home computers.

○ If you're familiar with the video game *Minecraft* then you know, for many, it's much more than a game. That's probably why *Minecraft* is the top-selling game of all time, with more than 238 million units sold.

- Most of the world's computer-integrated circuit (IC) chips are made in semiconductor fabrication plants owned by Taiwan based companies. Taiwan companies accounted for more than 60% of the market share in 2020.

- Python was the most widely used computer language in 2021. It was first developed in 1991 by a Dutch programmer, Guido van Rossum.

- Lenovo was the top-selling computer brand in 2020, with 87 million units sold and 19% of the market share. Apple was second with 81.4 million units sold and 18% of the market.

- The abacus was the world's first calculator. Variations of the device were used as far back as the 3rd millennium BCE in Mesopotamia.

- A multiple arcade machine emulator (MAME) is software that emulates vintage arcade games. The software is legal in most countries and is also open source.

- A "killer app" is computer software that's deemed so cool or essential that people buy specific hardware just to run the application. The spreadsheet program VisiCalc for the Apple II is considered the first computer killer app.

- In 2000, the Windows Mobile phone was the first true smartphone to hit the market. The platform was declared "end of life" on January 14, 2020.

- A "binary digit," or bit, is the basic unit of information in computing. A "byte" is a unit that generally consists of 8 bits.

- "5G" stand for "fifth generation" cellular network. It's estimated that there will be 1.7 billion 5G subscribers by 2025.

- The Internet has been around in different forms since the 1970s, but the World Wide Web was invented in 1989 by British computer scientist Tim Berners-Lee.

- The Atari 2600 console hit the stores in 1977. It was a big step up from previous game systems because it used separate cartridges for each game.

- The iPhone was first released to the public on June 29, 2007, while the Android mobile operating system was released by Google on September 23, 2008.

- "Techies" are often referred to as "nerds." The oldest documented use of the word nerd is in the 1950 Dr. Suess book *If I Ran the Zoo*.

○ Brothers Sam and Dan Houser, Jamie King, and Terry Donovan started Rockstar Games on January 22, 1999. The company is responsible for creating the popular *Grand Theft Auto* franchise.

○ Asus computers are made by ASUSTek Computer Inc. based in Taipei, Taiwan. Asus is relatively new to the field, being founded in 1989.

○ Atari made many of its own games for its console, including *E.T. the Extra-Terrestrial* in 1982. Atari ordered production of five million units of *E.T.* based on movie sales, but only sold 1.5 million copies.

FASCINATING FACTS OF
CHILDREN'S STORIES

○ Jacob (1785–1863) and Wilhelm (1786–1859) Grimm are usually known collectively as the "Brothers Grimm." The Brothers Grimm are best known for their retelling of European folktales, such as "Cinderella" and "Snow White."

○ The lyrics of the nursery rhyme "Ring around the Rosie" are a bizarre mystery. Many believe it refers to a bout of the plague where people carried bouquets of flowers & herbs to smell while walking in public, while others think it refers to a pagan ritual.

- Author Maurice Sendak based the wild thing creatures in his 1963 book, *Where the Wild Things Are*, on members of his extended family. He saw the members as "grotesque."

- There are more than 250,000 references to 25,000 English language folk songs in the Roud Folk Song Index. The database was started by librarian Steve Roud to collect as much information as possible about English folk tales from around the world.

- Italian writer Giambattista Basile (1566-1632) was one of the first collectors of folk and fairy tales in Western Europe. Tales attributed to Basile include "Verde Prato" and "The She-Bear."

- The oldest collection of published nursery rhymes is *Tommy Thumb's Song Book*. Published in 1774, the book contains such classics as "London Bridge" and "Patty Cake."

- The children's game "Duck, Duck, Goose" is called "Duck, Duck, Gray Duck" in the state of Minnesota. The person tagged "gray duck" is the one who does the chasing.

- "Pattycake" is one of the oldest surviving English nursery rhymes. The earliest known recorded version of it is in the 1698 play, *The Campaigners*, by Thomas D'Urfey.

- Popular American writer, S.E. Hinton, whose novels often dealt with teens and their struggles, hit it big while she was still a teen. Hinton was only 18 when *The Outsiders* was published in 1967.

- You probably know the late Theodor Seuss Geisel by his penname, Dr. Suess. His first children's book was in 1937, *And to Think That I Saw It on Mulberry Street*.

- "Puss in Boots" was originally an Italian fairytale called "Il gatto con gli stivali." The original story involved the cat extorting innocent villagers and tricking the princess into believing his master was a noble.

- Humpty Dumpty is usually portrayed as an egg in visual versions of the nursery rhyme, but the words never state he was. Some historians believe Humpty Dumpty was simply a device for a riddle around breakable things. Others have suggested that Humpty Dumpty is King Richard III of England, who is supposed to have been humpbacked and who was defeated at the Battle of Bosworth Field in 1485.

- The earliest documented mention of the name "Mother Goose" is dated to the 1600s. Since she is associated with folk nursery rhymes, the character is likely much older.

- Clifford the Big Red Dog was the main character in 80 children's books. Interestingly, Clifford's size frequently changed, although he was usually 25 feet tall.

- Danish fairytale writer, Hans Christian Anderson (1805-1875) suffered serious injuries when he fell out of bed at the age of 67. His final publication, a collection of stories, appeared the same year. Around this time, he started to show signs of liver cancer that would take his life. He never fully recovered and died at the age of 70.

- Many believe that the nursery rhyme "Mary, Mary Quite Contrary" refers to Mary, Queen of Scots. Even more interesting, the "silver bells and cockle shells" may have referenced torture devices. No proof has been found that the rhyme was known before the 18th century, while Mary I of England (Mary Tudor) and Mary, Queen of Scots (Mary Stuart), were contemporaries in the 16th century.

- The nursery song/rhyme "Ba Ba Blacksheep" was the first song to be digitally saved and played on a computer. The recording took place in 1952 at the University of Manchester, UK.

- In the 1600s, "Humpty Dumpty" was the name of an alcoholic drink, but by the 1700s it was slang for an egg-shaped person.

- American writer, Laura Elizabeth Ingalls Wilder, who's best known for her *Little House on the Prairie* books, got her first start writing for the small-town paper the *Missouri Ruralist* in 1911. Her columns, much like her books, focused on farms and family.

- One of the most popular Japanese fairy tales is "Momotaro," or the "Peach Boy." In the story, Momotaro was born from a peach but became a demon-fighting hero.

- The 1806 book *Rhymes for the Nursery*, which was written by Jane and Anny Taylor, is believed to be the oldest use of the term "nursery rhyme."

- Many children's books use anthropomorphic animals and characters, but Richard Scarry developed an entire world of them. Scarry published over 300 children's books, but his best-remembered ones revolve around the animal inhabited city of "Busytown."

○ British children's book author, Roald Dahl, who wrote the 1964 novel, *Charlie and the Chocolate Factory*, served as an RAF fighter pilot during World War II.

○ The nursery rhyme "Mary Had a Little Lamb" originated in the US in the early 1800s. The rhyme was the first audio recorded on Thomas Edison's phonograph in 1877.

○ The Dr. Suess book *Green Eggs and Ham* uses only 50 unique words. Suess's publisher bet him that he couldn't write a book with only 50 words.

ALMOST RICH AND FAMOUS

○ Nineteen-year-old British woman, Rachael Kennedy, found out what it's like to almost have a fortune in 2021. Kennedy had all the right numbers to win the £182/$237 million pot, but she didn't have the funds in her lottery automatic payment account!

○ The quote, "In the future, everyone will be world-famous for 15 minutes" is often attributed to eccentric American artist Andy Warhol, but its origins are a bit obscure.

○ Tracii Guns was one of the founders of the 1980s rock ban, Guns N' Roses. He left in 1983, later stating that "it just wasn't fun anymore."

○ More than 200 people falsely claimed to be responsible for the Lindbergh baby kidnapping in 1932. Most were fame seekers.

○ Texas lawyer and political donor Harry Whittington kept a low profile until February 11, 2006, when US Vice President Dick Cheney shot and wounded him in a hunting accident.

○ In 2006, Harvard student Kaavya Viswanathan looked poised for a lucrative career as a writer when her book *How Opal Mehta Got Kissed, Got Wild, and Got a Life* was published. It turned out large portions were plagiarized, ending Viswanathan's writing career.

○ Money and fame/recognition are cited in many studies as two of the most common motivating factors in people's lives.

○ Dik (aka Dick) Evans was one of the founding members of the band, Feedback. The other members thought Evans was too old, so they fired him and changed their name to U2.

○ In 1961, little known brothers Richard McDonald and Maurice McDonald sold their small southern California chain of hamburger restaurants they called "McDonalds" to entrepreneur Ray Kroc for $2.7 million.

- Pete Best was the original drummer for the Beatles but was fired in 1962. The Beetles then invaded America and Best went on to form the long-forgotten 'The Pete Best Four'.

- Filippo Bernardini impersonated A-list literary agents to steal manuscripts from best-selling authors. The case is ongoing, but the authorities still haven't determined a motive.

- In February 2021, Timothy Wilks was shot and killed when he pulled a knife on David Starnes in Nashville, Tennessee as part of a YouTube robbery "prank." Wilks became neither famous nor wealthy.

- A man named Hubert Chang claims he was one of Google's original designers. So far, acknowledged founders Sergey Brin and Larry Page aren't saying much.

- An elementary school teacher named John Mark Karr became famous in 2006 when he confessed to murdering toddler model JonBenet Ramsey in 1996. The confession was proven to be false, likely done by Karr to become famous.

- The Apple computer company was founded in 1976 by Steve Jobs, Steve Wozniak, and Ronald Wayne. Wayne is often forgotten because he sold his share of 10% a few weeks later for $2,300.

- Career criminal Sante Kimes and her son Kenneth Kimes Jr. often impersonated other people in fraud schemes. Sante often claimed to be Elizabeth Taylor, although she didn't look much like her.

- Thomas Dewey had a successful career as a federal prosecutor and governor of New York from 1943 to 1954, but he's best known for losing the 1948 presidential election to Harry Truman.

- Teen brothers Robert and Michael Bever stabbed and beat to death five members of their family in Broken Arrow, Oklahoma on July 22-23, 2015. Two members of the family, a 2-year-old girl and a 13-year-old girl survived, the latter of whom identified two of her older brothers, 18-year-old Robert Bever and 16-year-old Michael Bever, as the assailants. The motive for their horrific crimes was fame.

- The American TV comedy skit show, *Turn-On*, only broadcast one complete episode in many markets on February 5, 1969, with the second episode canned. Today, it's difficult to find the complete first episode.

- In 1982 a petty criminal named Michael Fagan snuck into the Queen's bedroom in Buckingham Palace. Fagan's feat was quickly forgotten by the press.

○ Everyone knows who Mark Zuckerberg is, but twins Cameron and Tyler Winklevoss are far less famous. The former Olympic rowers are best known for accusing Mark Zuckerberg of stealing their idea for a social network. They used some of their $65 million legal settlement with the Facebook CEO to start stockpiling Bitcoin. The twins still own an estimated 70,000 Bitcoins, in addition to other digital assets.

○ The 17th US President, Andrew Johnson, was impeached in 1868 but staved off conviction by one vote. If he had been convicted, the presidency would've passed to Benjamin Wade.

○ Personal trainer Greg Anderson almost became famous for providing steroids to MLB player Barry Bonds. On July 15, 2005, Anderson, in a deal with federal prosecutors, pleaded guilty to conspiracy to distribute steroids and to money laundering. On October 18, 2005, he was sentenced by U.S. District Court Judge Susan Illston to three months in prison and three months' home confinement.

○ In 2011, a Georgia convenience store sold a Powerball lottery ticket worth $77 million. No one ever came forward to claim the prize.

○ Shawn Fanning and Sean Parker were at the top of the tech game in early 1999 with Napster. Less than two years later they were all but forgotten thanks to several lawsuits.

URBAN MYTH FACTS

○ Many people in Central America believe in a canine creature known as El Cadejo. It's a creature that can be benevolent or malevolent. In some countries, El Cadejo is also said to move more like a deer than a dog. In some versions of the story, the creature is also said to be dragging a chain that wraps around its neck. In fact, some claim that the word "cadejo" comes from the Spanish word for "chain."

○ In Llangernyw, Wales, some locals think that a creature called the Angelystor holds the secrets of life and death. The inhabitants of the small village say their local church is haunted by the spirit of Angelystor. Located on the grounds of the church is the oldest living tree in Wales, which is believed to have begun growing in the Bronze Age. Each year on Halloween and on the 31st of July, Angelystor is said to appear beneath the tree and announces in Welsh (rather grimly we may add) the name of the parish members who will die shortly

○ The "Black Volga" was an urban myth popular in the Eastern Bloc. The myth stated that mysterious men drove a black Volga limousine, abducting unsuspecting children.

○ It's believed that the term "urban myth" was first used by American folklorist, Richard Dorson, in 1968.

○ One myth states that temporary tattoos for kids have been soaked in LSD. Usually, the sticker is a "blue star," although variations are common, no documented case has ever been reported.

○ One unhelpful urban myth is that typing the PIN on your ATM card backwards will summon the police. Don't bother trying it!

○ In 1959, a California dentist named William Shyne handed out laxative laced candy for Halloween. Many believe that this case gave rise to the urban myth of razor blades being placed in candy.

- There's a persistent myth that when Walt Disney died in 1966 either his head or his whole body was cryogenically frozen and stored at one of the Disney theme parks.

- US Congressman, Hale Boggs Sr. from Alaska mysteriously disappeared on October 16, 1972, on a flight from Anchorage to Juneau. Some think he was the victim of the "Alaska Triangle."

- Professor Jan Harold Brunvand introduced the public to the term "urban myth" with his 1981 collection of urban myths, *The Vanishing Hitchhiker: American Urban Legends & Their Meanings*.

- Although it's an urban myth that baby alligators flushed down toilets have grown to full size, rats can and have swum up through the pipes in toilets!

- Legendary actor Charlie Chaplin allegedly entered a Chaplin look-alike contest and came in 20th. Other versions of the myth have him placing higher, but he never wins.

- The rabbit-antelope hybrid, jackelope, is a mythical animal associated with the states of South Dakota and Wyoming. The origins of the creature are unknown, but the locals love it!

- In the early 1980s, gamers thought there was an arcade game called *Polybius* that was controlling the players' minds. The myth obviously combined elements of CIA black ops with the arcade craze of the era.

- An urban myth holds that seven gates in rural Hellam Township, Pennsylvania guard the entrance to Hell, but the locals aren't so sure. Trespassers have been arrested trying to find out.

- The activity of "Cow tipping" is an urban myth. Cows frequently lay down and can easily get back up.

- "Creepypasta" are scary stories and memes that have been cut and pasted and shared on the Internet. Some creepypasta stories are urban legends, while others are memes.

- In 2016, there was a rash of "evil clown" sightings throughout the US and Canada as well as 18 other countries. Why the sightings began, and suddenly ended, remains a mystery.

- Urban myths and legends are quite popular in Japan. Most Japanese urban legends focus on ghosts, *yūrei*, rarely featuring monsters.

○ If you go to the URL www.blindmaiden.com you'll be sent to a blank page. But according to one urban myth, if you go there at the right time you'll be attacked by a blind woman.

○ A "snipe hunt" is a part urban legend and part practical joke. Although there are birds called snipes, a "snipe hunt" is usually a practical joke done to people not familiar with the outdoors.

○ Before evil clown sightings were a thing, in 1970 the residents of Fairfax County, Virginia reported seeing an axe-wielding man in a bunny costume stalking the area. The bunny was never captured.

○ Coca-Cola is acidic and isn't very good for you, but it isn't used by the police to clean blood from crime scenes. Coke also isn't powerful enough to dissolve flesh and bones.

○ John Gilchrist, the actor who played Mikey in the "Life" serial commercials in the 1970s, didn't die from eating a pop rock.

○ Legendary bluesman Robert Johnson died after drinking poisoned whiskey in a juke joint on August 16, 1938, at the age of 27. His death was never reported and in the following decades, his life turned into an urban myth, including how he sold his soul to the devil to learn the blues.

FURNITURE FACTS

○ American company Steelcase was the leading furniture manufacturer in the world in 2020. The company has approximately 80 locations and 11,000 employees worldwide. Steelcase primarily makes office furniture.

○ The bean bag chair was invented in 1968 by Italian designers Piero Gatti, Cesare Paolini, and Franco Teodoro. Its popularity peaked in the late 1970s.

○ It's believed the earliest furniture was constructed in the Mesolithic Period (20,000-8,000 years ago) or the early Neolithic Period (ca. 120,000-4,500 years ago). They were made from wood, stone, and animal bones.

○ Thomas Chippendale (1718-1779) was a cabinet maker who combined furniture styles of his era to create a new style known as "Chippendale." He also designed the homes of the British elite.

○ American company Ashley HomeStore is the top retail furniture store in sales in the US. Close at number two is Swedish founded, Dutch headquartered, IKEA.

○ In 2020, China was the world's leading exporter of furniture, with $69 billion worth. Poland was second with nearly $13 billion worth of furniture exports.

○ Although the Romans didn't invent the sofa, they knew how to use them! Roman patricians enjoyed lounging on sofas while they entertained guests, who would also have had sofas to lounge on.

○ American tycoon, Warren Buffett, got into the furniture business in 1983 when his Berkshire Hathaway bought Nebraska Furniture Mart for $60 million. Berkshire later bought other furniture chains.

○ Early bookshelves held papyrus scrolls, so they looked a bit different. It wasn't until after the Guttenberg Press was invented in the 1430s that books as we know them were created, requiring a true bookshelf.

○ Staying true to their Swedish roots, IKEA also sells meatballs. IKEA sells about 150 million meatballs every year.

○ The ancient Egyptians didn't use pillows. The Egyptians used headrests, which all but ensured that a person would have to sleep on their back.

○ The average sofa gets 2,958 days of use, or just over eight years before it gets sent to the curb.

○ The futon was developed in Japan. Traditionally, Japanese futons are placed on top of a matting called *tatami*.

○ Mayflower Transit, better known in the US as "Mayflower Moving," was founded by Conrad M. Gentry and Don F. Kenworthy in Indianapolis, Indiana in 1927. The company is an agent-owned cooperative.

○ The finest Egyptian furniture was made from ebony. Since ebony had to be imported from the African interior, it was more valuable.

○ The "Badminton Cabinet" twice set the record for the most expensive piece of furniture ever sold. Built in 1726 for the 3rd Duke of Beaufort, the Cabinet was last sold by Christie's in 2004 for £19 million (approx.) $36.7 million.

○ Although some believe a young Benjamin Franklin made the first rocking chair, its inventor will probably never be known. First designed in America, rocking chairs began being sold in England in 1725.

- When North American plains Indians needed to move, they packed up their belongings on a framed structure called a *travois*. A travois could be attached to a horse, dog, or human and then *dragged*, as it had no wheels.

- Allied Van Lines is the oldest moving company in the US. It was founded in 1928, just before Mayflower began service.

- IKEA claims that its "Billy" bookcase is the most commercially successful piece of furniture. More than 110 million Billy cases have been sold in the last 40 years.

- The modern word "table" is derived from the ancient Latin word *tabula*. A Roman tabula could be any flat piece of board and didn't have to have four legs.

- As Charles Darwin (1809-1882) developed his theory of evolution, he also invented the modern office chair by adding wheels to make a swiveling chair.

- Irish furniture designer Eileen Gray's (1878-1976) financial masterpiece was the "Dragons" armchair created from 1917 to 1919. The chair sold for just under 22 million euros (about 23 million dollars) in 2009.

- "Rustic" furniture is any future that uses wood to give the finished product a "natural" and "country" look. Using pallets/skids to make furniture is a recent rustic trend.

- The modern word "ebony" is likely derived from the ancient Egyptian word for the wood, *hebony*. The Greeks then called the wood, *ebenos*.

WEAPONS OF WAR

○ Dogs have been used as weapons throughout history. In World War II, the Soviets used them as suicide bombers and more recently North Korea has trained dogs for similar missions.

○ The Germans developed remote-controlled bombs during World War II known as "Goliath tracked mines." Germany produced 7,564 single-use Goliaths during the war.

○ The earliest depictions of siege weapons were rendered by Assyrian artists in the 9th and 8th centuries BCE. A common Assyrian weapon was the mobile siege tower.

○ The Tsar Tank was first developed in Imperial Russia in 1914, but the project was cancelled in 1915. The "tank" was essentially a giant tricycle on wheels, which I guess is why its production was cancelled.

○ The US Military is currently working on a pulsed energy projectile or PEP, which uses a laser to send small amounts of exploding plasma. The Military claims this will be a non-lethal weapon.

○ Kevlar, the synthetic fiber used in bullet-resistant clothing, was invented by American chemist Stephanie Louise Kwolek in 1965.

○ The primary weapon the Roman centurions used was a one-handed sword called a *gladius*. Gladius was also the Latin word for any sword.

○ Although the ancient Egyptians were master chariot fighters, the vehicle/weapon wasn't invented by them. The chariot was brought to Egypt by invaders known as the Hyksos sometime around 1650 BCE.

○ Robert Mainhardt and Art Biehl invented the gyrojet class of guns/small arms in the early 1960s. These weapons shot mini rockets called "Microjets."

○ In 1998, the US Army began developing the "vortex ring gun." The gun is a nonlethal weapon that shoots vortex rings of gas, capable of knocking a person to the ground.

- The M4A1 carbine is the standard issue rifle for the US Army. It began replacing the M16 in 2010.

- The urumi is a unique weapon that originated in India. It's a four to five feet long thin, a bladed weapon that looks like and is used as a whip.

- An airborne laser is a laser fitted on a jet that's used to destroy missiles. High costs led to the US scrapping its airborne lasers, but the Russians still have two active laser laboratories.

- The "Parthian shot" was a tactic made famous by the Parthians (247 BCE-CE 224), The Parthian shot is a light cavalry hit-and-run tactic made famous by the Parthians, an ancient Iranian people. While performing a real or feigned retreat at full gallop, the horse archers would turn their bodies back to shoot at the pursuing enemy.

- As a nod to their love of scooters, the French military developed the Vespa 150 TAP for the special forces in the 1950s. The scooter came with a 75 mm recoilless rifle!

- Soviet general, Mikhail Timofeyevich Kalashnikov, is best known as the inventor of the AK-47 rifle. But Kalashnikov had a soft side, writing poetry and six books.

- In 2005, some nerds with NASA created the BigDog - a quadruped military robot. The military quickly shelved the project when it was determined the robots were too loud.

- In the last nine months of World War II, the Japanese unleashed Fu-Go "bomb balloons" on the US. Hundreds of incendiary balloons were launched from Japan, but only six Americans died in the attacks and very little physical damage was done.

- Due to their high intelligence and affable nature, dolphins have been trained by the militaries of Russia and the US for many tasks, including bomb detection.

- The cat o' nine tails was a weapon used by the British militaries (primarily in the Navy) against their own insubordinate troops. The weapon was a two- to a three-foot-long leather strap that had nine knotted thongs of cotton cord at the ends.

- In 1718, Englishman James Puckle patented the world's first machine gun. The revolutionary weapon never saw combat, though, and as few as two were produced.

○ For much of ancient Egyptian history (ca. 3,000-1275 BCE), the Egyptian infantry used a 20 inch long, sickle-shaped, slashing sword called a khepesh.

○ The Cho-ko-nu was a repeating crossbow that was invented in China during the Warring States Period (475–220 BCE). It could shoot ten bolts in under 30 seconds.

○ Although the AK-47 is one of the most popular military weapons in the world, it's also the most copied. The Kalashnikov company didn't patent their rifle until 1997.

○ The personnel halting and stimulation response rifle (PHASR) is a non-lethal rifle that's been developed by the US Airforce and is in the prototype stage. It works by temporarily blinding the target with a laser.

YOU CAN COUNT ON IT

○ The largest known prime number has 24,862,048 digits when written in base 10. It was "discovered" by Patrick Laroche in 2018.

○ The concept of zero seems so simple, but few pre-modern people developed it. The Indians were the first people to develop the zero as a written digit maybe in the 7th century CE but possibly earlier.

○ In geometry, a polygon is any shape that has a limited/finite number of straight lines that close together to form the shape. Triangles and squares are polygons, but circles are not because their lines are not straight.

○ If you multiple the number nine by any number, and add all the digits of the sum, you'll always get nine. For instance, 127x9=1,143; 1+1+4+3=9. It's true every time!

○ The ancient Egyptians and ancient Egyptians had symbols for and used fractions in their math, but they did so without the concept of zero.

○ "Combinatorics" refers to any type of counting. Although it sounds simple enough, combinatorics includes probability, finite geometry, and design theory.

○ The study known as "game theory" combines math with social science, logic, and computer science. It's generally used to determine what a person's losses or gains will be in a particular scenario.

○ The ancient Greek mathematician, Pythagoras (ca. 570-495 BCE), is best known for his theorem - $a^2+b^2=c^2$ - but he was also a mystic who led a commune.

○ "I'll be back in a jiffy" actually refers to time measurement. In computer animation, a jiffy represents 1/100th-of-a-second, while in electronics it's a period of an alternating current power cycle; either 1/60 or 1/50 of a second.

○ A "quant" is a person who uses quantitative analysis in financial investing. The investment methods quants use is often called quantitative investment management.

- Economics is the study of the exchange of goods, services, and commodities. Although you don't have to be a math whiz to be an economist, the study does require some algebra, calculus, and statistics.

- A picture within a picture, etc., is known as the "Droste effect." Theoretically, this could continue infinitely but in practicality, it only continues as long the image can be seen.

- The double-entry system of bookkeeping or accounting is often attributed to the Florentine merchant, Amatino Manucci. His double-entry accounts from 1299-1300 are the earliest on record.

- The opposite sides of traditional dice always add up to seven. You can throw the dice as much as you want, but it's always the case.

- Complex analysis is a type of math that concerns how complex numbers function. Mechanical, electrical, and nuclear engineering all use complex analysis, such as determining how to launch a satellite.

- Did you know that you can always cut through a ham and cheese sandwich so that the remaining halves are exactly the same size? This is called the ham sandwich theorem.

- There are 52 cards in a traditional deck of cards and 52! (Factorial 52) permutations of those cards. That number is …

- 80658175170943878571660636856403766975289505440883327782400000 0000000.

- The number system most people use today is the Arabic numerals. Europeans used the clumsier Roman numeral system until they realized how much easier Arabic numerals were by the mid-1500s.

- The number googol is written as the digit "1" followed by 100 zeroes. The founders of Google chose that name because it was a common misspelling of googol.

- The math used by the ancient Egyptians and Mesopotamians was practical but not abstract. Their math didn't have mathematical proofs, which were first developed by the Greeks.

- According to the "birthday problem," 23 random people can be placed in a room and there's a 50% chance two of them will have the same birthday.

○ A zero-sum game is a game theory application where there are two sides with finite resources available. The more resources one side gets will result in an equivalent loss for the other side.

○ The smallest measure of time in ancient Egypt was the *at*. Although *at* has no definite span, it's usually translated as "moment."

○ "Forty" is the only number that's spelt in alphabetical order in English. Four is also the only number that has the same number of letters as the number itself.

○ The Maya and Chinese also understood the concept of zero. The Maya often represented zero as an empty tortoise shell in their hieroglyphic script.

ALL KINDS OF HOBBIES, STRANGE OR OTHERWISE

○ If you like extreme sports and are picky about wearing neatly pressed clothes, then extreme ironing may be the hobby for you. Extreme ironers iron their clothes on mountain tops and at the bottom of lakes – and even on surfboards!

○ Insect fighting is a popular pastime in parts of Asia. Cricket fighting is the thing in China, while the Japanese prefer to fight beetles.

○ Quidditch is a real-life game/sport that was taken from the fictional *Harry Potter* franchise. Real quidditch was first played in 2005 in Middlebury, Vermont.

○ A *bibliophile* is a person who loves to read and collect books. The book is derived from the Greek words *biblio* "book" and *phile* "love."

○ The ancient Assyrians loved to hunt lions. Some sculpture reliefs from the palace of King Ashurbanipal (669-631 BCE) depict the king hunting lions, even with his bare hands.

○ Geocaching is where people use GPS to locate a small prize buried somewhere outdoors. The first geocaching event took place on May 3, 2000, in Beavercreek, Oregon.

○ The sport of wife-carrying is big in Finland. In this activity, men race through an obstacle course while carrying a female teammate.

○ More than three million chess boards are sold every year in the US alone, making it the best-selling board game of all time. Not bad for a game that dates back to 1200!

○ Noodling is catfish fishing with your bare hands. Due to dangers, such as drowning, noodling is illegal in most US states.

○ Playing with mudballs is considered an artform in Japan. *Hikaru dorodango* is a Japanese art form in which earth and water are molded, and then carefully polished to create a delicate shiny sphere, resembling a billiard ball

○ J.C. Payne took knitting to a whole new level by creating the *Guinness Book of World Record's* largest ball of twine. It measures 41.5 feet in circumference. There are multiple claims to the world's biggest ball of twine record in the United States. As of 2014, the ball of twine with the largest circumference is located in Cawker City, Kansas

○ The residents of Castrillo de Murcia, Spain celebrate the feast of Corpus Christi by jumping over babies. The festival, which is to ward off the devil, began in 1620.

○ You have to be a nerd and a jock to chessbox. As the name indicates, the sport involves playing chess *and* boxing. Chessboxers must have competed in 50 amateur boxing matches and have an Elo (chess) rating of 1600.

○ When North Carolina dermatologist Manfred Rothstein wasn't working, he was collecting back scratchers. In 2008 he became the world record holder with 675 back scratchers from 71 different countries.

○ The largest ice fishing contest in the world is held on Gull Lake in Minnesota every January. The contest attracts more than 15,000 people every year.

- The world's first board game was the ancient Egyptian game of *senet*. Although several senet boards have been discovered, none of them came with directions!

- The most expensive board game ever sold was a 23-carat gold Monopoly game made by the jeweler, Sidney Mobell. The gold Monopoly board sold for a cool $2 million!

- Frenchman David Belle is considered the father of the sport/activity, parkour. Parkour involves a variety of athletic skills and is heavily influenced by military obstacle course running.

- "Randonautica" is an app that supposedly randomly generates local coordinates for users to check out their area. In late 2020, the coordinates sent one group to the location of two corpses. The app's founder claims it was purely a coincidence.

- American trophy hunters took nearly 43% of their trophies from Canada from 2005 to 2014. The second most popular trophy origin country was South Africa, with 32%.

- In 2021, a new "hobby" started on TikTok called "devious licks." It consisted of crimes being committed and then posted on TikTok. Yes, plenty of arrests were made!

- "Dark tourism" is where tourists purposely visit the scenes of massacres, genocides, and/or serial killings. One of the most controversial was a $10 tour to see all of Jeffrey Dahmer's former haunts in Milwaukee, Wisconsin.

- Falconry has been primarily a hobby of the nobility and elites throughout the world. The earliest records of falconry can be traced back to 2000 BCE in Mesopotamia.

- According to the *Guinness Book of World Records*, Englishman David Morgan owns the largest collection of traffic cones. The collection includes 132 unique cones.

- The bass is the most popular freshwater game fish in the US. In addition to being fierce fighters, bass can be found in every region of the US.

FROM HOT TAMALES TO COLD COFFEE

○ Haggis may look like a slightly exotic hot pocket, but the Scottish fare is very different. It consists of a sheep's internal organs, onions, oatmeal, suet, and various spices, all packed inside a sheep's stomach!

○ Tamales are an ancient dish dating back at least 5,000 years in Mesoamerica. The word "tamale" is derived from the Nahuatl/Aztec word, *tamalli*.

○ In 1767, English chemist Joseph Priestley invented the process of carbonating water. From there, others added to the discovery until they arrived at the soda and beer of today.

○ The Arab chemist, Al-Kindi, made one of the earliest written references to the distillation of wine in the CE 800s. Brandy is created by distilling wine.

○ The mystery meat Spam is made in the heartland of the Midwest in Austin, Minnesota, but it's most popular in island locales. Spam is so popular in Hawaii it's served at McDonalds.

○ David A. Embry's *The Fine Art of Mixing Drinks*, published in 1948, became the world's first true cocktail guide, complete with recipes. There have been three editions of the book.

○ "Fry sauce" is a combination of ketchup and mayonnaise. It's a popular condiment in many of the US mountains states.

○ "Iced coffee" is a coffee drink served on ice, but it shouldn't be confused with cold brew coffee, which is the process of steeping coffee grounds in cold water.

○ The origin of the word "cocktail" is debated. Some believe it came from the Nahuatl word for flower, *xochitl*, while others think it comes from the rooster tails that were once served as garnishes with drinks.

○ Haiti and North Korea are tied with spirits being 97% of all alcohol consumed in their borders. I guess poverty and repression will do that to you!

- If you're in Japan, you may want to rethink ordering the "cherry blossom meat." It's the English translation of *sakuraniku*, which is raw horse meat.

- When Australian beer breweries are done with a batch, they take the stuff from the bottom of the barrel and make vegemite, which is a popular Australian sandwich spread.

- McDonald's is the top fast-food chain in the world in many locations, but the Yum! Brands - which include KFC, Taco Bell, and Pizza Hut - take in more revenue collectively.

- Kangaroo is the choice meat among some indigenous peoples in Australia. Some Australian companies will even ship kangaroo meat around the world but not to the State of California!

- North Americans call them French fries, or fries, while the British call them "chips." Most English speakers call a biscuit product "biscuits," but Americans call them "cookies."

- There's a chain of fast-food restaurants in the Philippines called Graceland. They serve traditional Filipino food and have nothing to do with Elvis Presley or Memphis, Tennessee.

- South Korean company, HiteJinro, is the top-selling spirit brand in the world. It produces beer and wine, but its signature item is its soju, which is a traditional Korean spirit.

- Lutefisk is a dried whitefish that is pickled in lye that was once quite popular in Scandinavia. It's known for its foul odor, gooey texture/consistency, and bland taste.

- Tequila doesn't come with a worm, that's mescal. And don't worry if you accidentally swallow the mescal worm because it isn't hallucinogenic.

- The term "bushmeat" generally refers to any wildlife hunted for food in Africa, but often refers to usually taboo meats such as primates, bats, and rodents.

- Most of the English-speaking world calls public drinking fountains "drinking fountains" or "water fountains," but in southern Wisconsin, Massachusetts, and Rhode Island they're known as "bubblers."

- Baijiu is a spirit that originated in China during the Ming Dynasty (30-50% alcohol). It's generally distilled from fermented sorghum, but also rice, wheat, or barley.

○ If you're ever in Sardinia and want to sample the local cuisine, you might want to take a pass on the *casu martzu*. Casu martzu is a dish of rotten goat cheese that contains live maggots!

○ Long before cola was a thing, sarsaparilla was the most popular soft drink in the 1800s. Sarsaparilla is a non-carbonated drink made from the smilax plant, which gives it a sugary taste.

○ Armenia is the location of the world's first winery. The Areni-1 winery is a cave complex where wine was made beginning around 4,100 BCE.

PLAGUED CORPSES, GREEK FIRE, AND MUSTARD GAS

○ Chemical and biological weapons have probably existed since the Pre-historic Era in one form or another. Poisoning an enemy's water supply is an early example.

○ It's believed Mongol armies brought the Black Death into Europe when they besieged the Genoese trading city of Kaffa on the Black Sea in 1347. The Mongols catapulted infected corpses into the city, spreading the disease.

○ Lewisite was a chemical weapon developed by the US government in 1917 for World War I. The war ended before any was used.

○ The Carthaginians reportedly catapulted pots filled with venomous snakes onto the ships of the Pergamon navy during a battle in 184 BCE.

○ The Biological Weapons Convention (BWC) is a treaty signed in 1972 that went into effect in 1975 prohibiting the production and use of biological weapons. Who has not signed the BWC? Ten states have neither signed nor ratified the BWC (Chad, Comoros, Djibouti, Eritrea, Israel, Kiribati, Micronesia, Namibia, South Sudan, and Tuvalu). The BWC opened for signature on April 10, 1972 and entered into force on March 26, 1975.

○ The first large-scale use of a chemical weapon on the battlefield took place on April 22, 1915, at the Second Battle of Ypres in Belgium. The Germans dispersed chlorine gas on the French, creating a temporary salient.

○ The Sassanian Persians defeated the Romans at the Siege of Dura-Europos in CE 256 through chemical warfare. The Persians dug tunnels under the city and ignited sulfur dioxide when the Romans attempted to enter one of the tunnels.

○ Scythian archers reportedly dipped their arrow heads in snake venom, rotting flesh, feces, or a combination of these. Their effectiveness is unknown.

- The Chemical Weapons Convention (CWC), which was signed in 1993 and went into effect in 1997, bans the production and use of chemical weapons. Only four countries have not ratified the agreement.

- Fort Detrick in Frederick, Maryland was the headquarters of the US biological weapons program from 1943 to 1969. After the BWC, it served as a center for "biological defense."

- Greek Fire was an incendiary, napalm-like weapon used by the Byzantine Empire from 672 to 1453. The ingredients and process to make Greek Fire remain a mystery.

- In World War I, the German troops that used the gas/chemical weapons were the Pioneer Regiment 35, while the French equivalent was called the Z Companies.

- The 2001 anthrax attacks took place in the US from September 18, 2001, to October 12, 2001. The deadly bacteria were mailed to targets, killing five people.

- Smoke was routinely used in warfare by pre-modern militaries. The Taino Indians of the Caribbean used smoke bombs against the Spanish in the 1500s.

- Chlorine and phosgene were chemical weapons that affect the respiratory tract. Phosgene was six times more deadly than chlorine and accounted for 85% of all chemical weapons deaths in World War I.

- Israel is not a signatory of the BWC. The nation is suspected of having a biological weapons program but has never publicly acknowledged it.

- Although the British possibly gave smallpox infected blankets to the Delaware Indians during the Siege of Fort Pitt in 1763, there are no other historical accounts of "smallpox" blankets.

- The Vietcong traps known as "punji sticks" were deadly enough, but they were often made deadlier when the VC guerillas tipped the sharpened sticks with plant poison, feces, or urine.

- Chemical weapons could be delivered two ways in World War I: canisters or shells. Canisters required stealth and favorable wind, while chemical shells required special cannons.

- Operation Ranch Hand was the codename of the US military's campaign to defoliate large areas of Vietnam from 1962 to 1971 using the chemical Agent Orange. It was a mixture of two deadly and dangerous herbicides.

○ Mustard gas, or sulfur mustard, is a vesicant that burns the skin. It was first deployed on the battlefield in 1917 during World War I by the Germans.

○ Napalm is simply the mixture of a flammable liquid and a gelling agent. The napalm used in most modern militaries is "napalm B."

○ Egypt, South Sudan, and North Korea have not signed the CWC. Israel has signed but not ratified it, leading many to believe it has a chemical weapons program.

○ The Hittites may have driven plague victims into enemy territory in the Levant in 1,324 BCE. Hittite King Suppiluliuma died from the same plague when infected Hittite soldiers returned.

○ Chemical warfare only accounted for 1% of total deaths in World War I. And only 4.3% of all gas casualties died compared to 24% for other weapons.

KEEP IT DOWN!

○ The sound of the Big Bang happened on such a low frequency that even if humans were around, they wouldn't have been able to actually hear it!

○ Synesthesia is a condition where people see different colors accompanying music and other sounds. It's estimated that 1% to 4% of the population has synesthesia.

○ Modern scientists believe the volcanic eruption on Mount Thera, Greece around 1,600 BCE measured seven on the Volcanic Explosivity Index (VEI). If so, it was the loudest sound in history.

○ Cats and dogs have an excellent sense of sound, but they're nothing compared to dolphins. Dolphins can hear sounds 15 miles away.

- A whip needs to travel faster than the speed of sound to make the cracking noise. That means a whip goes 767 miles per hour when it's cracked.

- Hearing loss is a global problem. According to the Hearing Health Foundation, the number of people with hearing loss is more than those with Parkinson's Disease, Epilepsy, Alzheimer's Disease, and Diabetes combined.

- Paleontologists aren't sure of the exact sounds dinosaurs made, but they probably included snorts, grunts, hisses, and roars, depending upon the species. The *Lambeosaurus* may have even made a honking noise due to the hollow crest on its head.

- Molecules are needed to produce sound and since there are no molecules in space, there's no sound in space. It kind of ruins the fun of *Star Wars* and *Star Trek*!

- The loudness of sound is measured in decibels. A typical car horn puts out 100-110 decibels, while a crying baby can belt out 115 decibels!

- The first sound film, or "talkie" as they were called at the time, was *The Jazz Singer* in 1927. Silent films continued to be produced into the 1930s.

- The Orfield Labs anechoic chamber in Minneapolis, Minnesota was listed as the "quietest place on Earth" in 2005 and 2013 by the *Guinness Book of World Records*.

- The *Alpheus* or pistol shrimp is only about two inches long when fully grown, but it's snapping claws can create 218 decibels of sound. That's right up there with whales!

- The Last Ice Age would have been very audible to those living near the glaciers. Just as they do today, the glaciers would have been notable for their crackling, gurgling, and booming noises.

- The atomic bombs dropped on the Japanese cities of Hiroshima and Nagasaki on August 6 and 9, 1945, respectively, reached 240 decibels.

- Infrasound is sound waves that register below what humans can hear. Homing pigeons can perceive infrasound, but how they use that for navigation is a mystery.

- A "humming" sound of unknown origin has plagued Taos, New Mexico for decades. Strangely, though, only 2% of the population can apparently hear this noise.

- The world's first musical instruments were heard in Mesopotamia and Egypt in about 2,800 BCE. Some of the early instruments included lyres, sistra, and cymbals.

- Tinnitus is an annoying ringing in the ears. According to the NIDCD Epidemiology and Statistics Program, 10% of Americans have experienced it in the last year.

- Hertz (Hz) is the measure of vibrations or sound waves per second. The range for humans to hear something is between 1,000 and 6,000 Hz.

- In the 500s BCE, the Greek colony, Sybaris, in Italy, passed one of the earliest known noise ordinances. It prohibited tinsmiths and roosters from the city limits.

- The ossicles is the collective name of the three bones in the middle ear: hammer, anvil, and stirrup. They are the three smallest bones in the human body, but without them, we'd be deaf.

- A massive earthquake hit the Greek island of Rhodes in 226 BCE that could be heard for miles. It was big enough to destroy a large statue called the Colossus of Rhodes.

- The eruption of Mount Krakatoa on August 26, 1883 is the loudest recorded sound in history. The eruption was measured at 310 decibels and could be heard more than 3,000 miles away!

- A 1965 study in the Maaban region of Ghana proved that loud noises, not aging, were usually the cause of hearing loss. The study also showed that loud noises raise blood pressure.

- Things got a lot louder in the 1990s. According to the World Forum for Acoustic Ecology, the noise of conversations between Americans increased ten decibels that decade.

PRETENDERS AND CONTENDERS

○ From 1598 to 1613, Russia experienced what is known as the "Time of Troubles." During this time, there were at least three pretenders to the throne known today as "False Dmitry." False Dmitry I (reigned 1605-1606) was the only one to successfully take the throne.

○ Louis Alphonse de Bourbon is currently living the good life as a member of the Spanish nobility, but that's not good enough. He claims to be the rightful king of France, Louis XX.

○ A Brazilian named Pedro Carlos is one of two claimants who has made claims to the Brazilian "throne." Although Carlos is descended from Brazil's last emperor, the monarchy ended in 1889!

○ When the Iron Curtain of communism descended over Eastern Europe after World War II, it ended many of Europe's monarchies, although claims are still made by their descendants.

○ The ancient Egyptian queen, Hatshepsut (ruled 1,479-1,458 BCE), ruled as a co-regent with her nephew Thutmose III (1,479-1,425 BCE). She made the incredible step of having herself crowned "king" and is depicted as such in art and texts.

○ The term "pretender" was made famous by Queen Anne of Great Britain, who referred to her half-brother, James Francis Edward Stuart, as such in 1708.

○ The 3rd century in Rome was a time of crisis when several pretenders come to the throne. The Imperial Roman era historical text, *Historia Augusta*, lists 30 pretenders.

○ In 1817, a woman named Mary Willcocks conned the people of Almondsbury, England into believing she was the Princess of Caraboo. After getting some free room and board, Mary moved to the US.

○ An "antipope" is a claimant to the papacy who was not properly elected by the College of Cardinals. Antipopes were frequent in the Middle Ages.

- When the communists came to power in Russia, they executed the royal family leaving no heirs. Well, Maria Vladimirovna claims the throne as a great-great-granddaughter of Tsar Alexander II.

- A wealthy Roman named Firmus attempted to overthrow Emperor Aurelian in CE 273 and may have been temporarily successful. If he did succeed, he only ruled for less than a year.

- A royal imposter is different from a pretender. Pretenders are usually of the nobility or royal family, while an imposter is usually a con-artist with no royal background.

- Although DNA has proven that the entire Romanov family was executed in 1918, there have been several imposters claiming to be family members and their non-existent descendants. Several women have claimed to be Anastasia.

- Another situation involves rival dynasties forming within the borders of the same country claiming separate areas of the country. These would be considered "contenders."

- From 1309 to 1376, Rome, or at least part of it, moved to Avignon, France. After the French crown conflicted with Rome, it established its own, sympathetic papacy.

- Napoleon III was actually the nephew of Napoleon. He claimed to be the legitimate Emperor of the French and was able to pull it off from 1852 to 1870.

- German-born Anna Anderson is probably the world's most famous royal imposter. From the 1920s until she died in 1984, she claimed to be the murdered Princess Anastasia Romanov of Russia.

- In 728 BCE, Egypt was divided among at least seven rival kings and chieftains. Many of these rival claimants were of Libyan descent.

- John Timothy Keehan, who in 1967 changed his name to Count Juan Raphael Dante, claimed he was of Spanish nobility. Never mind that Dante is an Italian name!

- The Byzantine Empire was extinguished in 1453 by the Ottoman Turks, but it didn't stop Spanish lawyer Eugenio Lascorz y Labastida from claiming to be heir to the throne until he died in 1962.

- In 1773, a Russian Cossack named Yemelyan Pugachev led a rebellion and claimed to be the late Tsar Peter III. Catherine the Great suppressed his rebellion and executed the fake Peter in 1775.

- Perhaps one of the most interesting Romanov claims came from a Filipino woman named Caty Peterson. Even with DNA, she still claims Anastasia was somehow her grandma.

- A man of mysterious origins named Šćepan Mali became the first and only Tsar of Montenegro in 1773. He got the throne by claiming to be Peter III of Russia.

- If the Hohenzollern Dynasty of Prussia is ever re-established, then Georg Friedrich will be its king. He's the heir of the last King of Prussia and a wealthy businessman.

- After the Ottoman Empire was replaced by the Republic of Turkey in 1922, several descendants of the Ottoman nobility have made claims to the sultanate. The most recent is a man named Harun Osman.

DRUGS, LEGAL AND OTHERWISE

○ The name "heroin" was coined by the German pharmaceutical company Bayer in the late 1800s. It was taken from the German word, *heroisch*, which means "strong" or "heroic."

○ The once quite popular benzodiazepine, Valium, was named for the Latin word *vale*, which means "goodnight." Valium is known to put people out for the night.

○ Scopolamine is often prescribed for motion sickness, but some have found more nefarious uses for it. There have been 50,000 cases of it used in Columbia alone where it's been used to render victims unconscious and rob them.

○ At the end of 2020, the global pharmaceutical industry was valued at $1.27 trillion. That's a big jump from 2001 when it was valued at *only* $390 billion!

○ Hallucinogenic psilocybin mushrooms were taken by many different American Indian peoples as part of religious rituals. The Aztecs even referred to one species as the "divine mushroom."

○ Nutmeg contains a chemical called myristicin that has psychoactive properties. Don't worry, though, most people have to ingest quite a bit to feel any kind of high.

○ Cockroaches are a common prescription for burns, ulcers, and tuberculosis in China and South Korea. Roaches are also a common ingredient in cosmetics in those countries.

○ It's commonly believed that the Netherlands was the first country to legalize recreational cannabis use, but Uruguay was the first to do so in 2013.

○ In the 1980s, ethnobotanist Wade Davis claimed that Haitian Voodoo zombies were created by a combination of tetrodotoxin from a pufferfish and bufotoxin from a toad. They were then "reanimated" with a natural drug, datura.

- The US FDA declared cigarettes as "drug delivery devices" in 1995. But in 2000, the Supreme Court ruled that the FDA couldn't regulate tobacco as a drug.

- Rimonabant is a prescription drug used to treat severe obesity that hit the European market in 2006 but was pulled in 2008. It caused depression in 10% and suicidal thoughts in 1% of patients.

- Johnson and Johnson is the largest pharmaceutical company in the world by market capitalization, at $473.06 billion. J&J was also the number one company in revenue in 2021.

- Heroin was marketed and sold as a cough suppressant in the US from 1895 until 1924. Congress realized that heroin did stop coughs, but it turned users into junkies.

- The opioid morphine gets its name from the Greek god of sleep, Morpheus. Will you take the blue or red pill?

- Dextromethorphan (DXM) is a compound found in many cough medicines, such as Robitussin DM. High enough doses of DXM can cause intoxication that is sometimes referred to as "Robo tripping."

- Pharmaceutical science as it's known today only dates back to the 1800s, but the earliest written prescriptions were made in ancient Mesopotamia and ancient Egypt.

- The CIA dosed at least hundreds of unknowing subjects with LSD as part of the MKUltra Project from 1953 to 1973. The project resulted in several deaths.

- Cannabis is the most popular illicit drug in the US, while number two is cocaine. Cocaine was only gradually made illegal in the early 1900s.

- About 5% of the US population has used prescription drugs recreationally. Opioids are the most popular, but tranquilizers like alprazolam/Xanax are also commonly used recreationally.

- Mescaline is a naturally occurring hallucinogenic drug that's harvested from the San Pedro cactus. The cactus is native to South America but can be grown in other places with a similar climate.

- "Polysubstance" use or abuse refers to the purposeful mixing of psychoactive drugs. John Belushi, River Phoenix, and Philip Seymour Hoffman all overdosed on a mix of drugs.

○ The legality of recreational cannabis in the Netherlands is somewhat complicated. Although use and sale has been decriminalized, the cultivation of plants is still technically illegal.

○ If you have severe insomnia, the doctor may prescribe Halcion for you. Halcion gets its name from the Greek word *halcyon*, which refers to calmness and quiet.

○ Chewing gum is only available by prescription in Singapore and only gum that's "therapeutic," such as nicotine gum, is allowed.

○ Jimsonweed was once used to alleviate asthma, but its side effects often ended further use. Intoxication can cause a frightening trip that's never described as fun or enlightening.

GAS, SOLID, AND LIQUID

○ 71% of the Earth's surface is covered by water, with over 96% of that in the oceans. Combined with the water underground and in the atmosphere, all of Earth's water would cover 332,500,000 cubic miles.

○ The iceberg that the Titanic hit in 1912 came from Greenland and was probably thousands of years old, possibly 100,000 years old.

○ "Brackish water" refers to a body of water that has more salinity (salt) than freshwater, but less salt than seawater. Any body of water with a salt content of greater than 30% is considered to be salt water.

○ Although it was once believed that all water on Earth arrived via comets and asteroids more than four billion years ago, many scientists now believe that the release of hydrogen inside the planet also played a role.

- Ice sculpting is a popular hobby in many cold-weather regions. Tools used range from hammers and chisels to chainsaws.

- Water is generally a good conductor of electricity, but that doesn't include pure water. Water only becomes a conductor when it dissolves substances around it.

- Water exists in three *properties* - solid, gas, and liquid - but within each property, it has multiple forms. For example, ice, frost, and snow are all different forms of solid water.

- An endorheic lake is a lake with no outlet to larger bodies of water and is usually saline. The Caspian Sea is the world's largest endorheic lake.

- There are debates over the number of Earth's oceans. Some scholars believe the Antarctic and Arctic oceans are outlets of the Pacific, Atlantic, and Indian oceans.

- Water has both cohesive and adhesive properties. The cohesion works by water being attracted to water, while the adhesion is how water is attracted to other substances.

- Lake Baikal in Siberia is the largest freshwater lake in the world by volume, comprising 23% of the world's freshwater. But Lake Superior in the US and Canada is the largest in surface area, covering 31,700 square miles.

- The hydrologic or water cycle has four primary stages: evaporation, condensation, precipitation, and runoff. There are several sub-stages within each of these.

- The Jupiter moons of Ganymede, Europa, and Callisto, and the Saturn moons of Enceladus and Titan are all thought to have oceans beneath their surfaces.

- It seems counterintuitive, but hot water freezes faster than cold water. Tanzanian game warden, Erasto Bartholomeo Mpemba, first noted the "Mpemba effect" in 1963. Is the Mpemba effect true? Under our definition of the Mpemba effect, akin to the definition in the 'original' paper by Mpemba & Osborne (in which they documented "the time for water to start freezing") we are forced to conclude that the 'Mpemba effect' is not a genuine physical effect and is a scientific fallacy.24 Nov 2016

- On January 12, 2007, a woman named Jennifer Strange died of water intoxication after drinking nearly two gallons of water as part of a radio contest, "Hold Your Wee for a Wii." She didn't win the prize.

○ The Ganges River in India is one of the most polluted bodies of water in the world thanks to normal industrial pollution, but also due to human remains. Yes, the Ganges is a holy river in Hinduism where human ashes are discarded.

○ The Persian Gulf has been known as such for centuries but in the 1960s the Arabic-speaking nations that border it began calling it the "Arabian Gulf," much to the chagrin of Iran.

○ The size of the Great Salt Lake fluctuates quite a bit. In the 1980s, it covered more than 3,300 square miles, but in 2021 it reached a record low point of 950 square miles.

○ Desalination is the process whereby saline (salt) is extracted from water, leaving usable water and brine. The principal drawback is that it uses immense amounts of energy.

○ Triple point is the state at which a substance is solid, liquid *and* gas. Water's triple point is when its temperature is 32.018 °F and its pressure is 611.657 pascals.

○ North Atlantic icebergs, like the one the Titanic hit, are very hard compared to regular ice, but they are still only 10% as hard as concrete.

○ Water is often called the "universal solvent" because it dissolves more substances than any other liquid. This means that wherever water goes, it carries with it, chemicals and substances.

○ The Minnesota River is rare because of the direction it flows. It flows southeast from Big Stone Lake to Mankato, Minnesota before bending northeast and emptying into the Mississippi River.

○ The pH scale is essentially based on the purity of water. A pH level below seven is acidic, while a pH above seven is a base. Seven is the pH level of pure water.

○ The Ogallala Aquifer sits beneath eight states of the Great Plains of the US. It covers an area of about 174,000 square miles, providing water for millions of people.

CRAZY LAWS

○ An 1872 Scottish law states that no one can be drunk when in charge of a cow, horse, carriage, or steam engine. It doesn't say anything about sheep, though.

○ Moore County, Tennessee is the home of Jack Daniel's distillery, but it's also a dry county.

○ The Victorian, Australia Summary Offences Act of 1966 makes it illegal to do a lot of things in public. The law states that if you fly a kite, or play a game in public that annoys someone, then it's illegal.

○ Most apparently strange and crazy laws from around the world probably served a purpose at one point but have since been largely forgotten within the often-arcane books of statutes that few people read. The authorities themselves are usually unaware of them.

○ Driving with a bear uncaged is illegal in Missouri. I guess there were lots of bears on the road at one time in the Show-Me State!

○ A fairly recent law (2011) makes it illegal to be shirtless in Barcelona, Spain. This one may make a lot of sense.

○ The United Arab Emirates is a pretty conservative place. It's illegal to swear, but also to send someone a middle finger emoji!

○ Blue laws are laws that ban certain events or activities on the Sabbath. These usually involve no liquor sales, but the sale of houseware was banned on Sundays in many US states until the 1980s.

○ The state of Arkansas has a law on the books that regulates how the name is pronounced. I guess they got tired of people calling it Ar-Kansas!

○ It's actually a fineable offense to build sandcastles in some countries. In some parts of Spain, Italy, and even the US, the authorities have cracked down on unruly castle builders!

○ High heeled shoes are only permitted in Carmel, California if the wearer gets a permit from city hall first.

- In 1969, the elected officials of Skamania County, Washington made it illegal to kill a legendary Bigfoot. The violation was originally a felony, but it was amended 15 years later to be a misdemeanor.

- The Chinese government banned reincarnation without government permission in 2007. The absurd law was primarily directed at Tibetan Buddhists and the Dalai Lama.

- Turkey is a little on the conservative side, which has influenced some of its alcohol laws. Boozing is banned on election day.

- The State of Oklahoma has some strange, obsolete laws that are still on the books. One of the most interesting is the law that prohibits simulated sex acts with buffaloes.

- Earlier, we saw how gum is only allowed with a prescription in Singapore. Even if you have a prescription, it's illegal to chew gum on Singapore's public transit.

- It's illegal in Alabama for "provocative" images to be shown on the labels of alcoholic drinks. It is, after all, the Bible Belt!

- Drunk driving is taken pretty seriously in nearly every country in the world, but not everywhere. The African nations of Niger, Togo, and The Gambia have no legal limit for intoxicated drivers.

- Self-service gas pumps are illegal in the states of Oregon and New Jersey. Oregon allows exceptions in counties of less than 40,000 people.

- In Louisiana, you can get fined for sending a pizza delivery driver to the wrong house. That law was obviously written before caller ID and smartphone apps.

- The beauty shop is such a relaxing place for many women. So much so that in Florida it's still technically illegal for a woman to fall asleep under a hairdryer.

- In the mid to late 1800s, attempts were made to use camels in the American west. Apparently, the people of Nevada didn't like it because they banned the ungulates from the state's highways.

- Single women in La Paz, Bolivia can drink as much booze as they like, but married women may only have one drink.

- It's illegal to climb trees in Toronto, Ontario and it's also verboten to swear in that city's public parks. After all, Canadians are nothing if not polite people!

- Sharing your Netflix password is punishable by a $2,500 fine and up to a year in jail in the state of Tennessee.

WHAT'S IN A NAME?

○ There's a town in New York and one in Ontario named Swastika as well as a lake in Wyoming and a mountain in Oregon. The swastika was a popular symbol long before the Nazis appropriated it.

○ Although Eric II, King of Norway (ruled 1280-1299), was nominally a Christian, he had problems with the Church. So, he earned the nickname "Priest Hater." Why did people in Norway not like Eric Bloodaxe? Eric's rule was reputedly harsh and despotic and so he fell rapidly out of favour with the Norwegian nobility.

○ "Bald Knob" is always good for a chuckle or two when you pass one on the highway. There are two towns named Bald Knob in the US and one in Australia.

○ "Grant Balfour" isn't the best name if you're a baseball pitcher. Still, Grant Balfour not only had a nice career as a Major League pitcher, but he's also the all-time save and strikeout leader among Australian MLB players.

○ What Cheer, Iowa is notable for its name but little else. The town was given the name in 1865, although the reason for it is debated. Population 607 in 2020.

○ If you travel through County Essex, England, you may visit the village of Ugley. And if you go a few more miles to the west to County Herefordshire, you'll end up in the hamlet of Nasty.

○ A *nom de plume* is just a fancy, French term for a "pen name." Many notable authors have used them, including Stephen King, who sometimes wrote as "Richard Bachman."

○ Swastika Mukherjee is the name of a popular Indian actress born in 1980. The word *swastika*, as well as the symbol, goes back to India more than 3,500 years ago.

○ Lancaster County, Pennsylvania is home to the towns of Intercourse, Paradise, and Blue Ball, which is interesting considering it's the heart of Amish country.

- Halfdan the Mild was a Viking king who got his nickname for being stingy with food but generous with gold. His father was Eystein Halfdansson, or Eystein Fret.

- Embarrass, Minnesota gets its unique name from the French word, *embarrass*, which means "to hinder with obstacles or difficulties." Apparently, even the hearty voyageurs found the town's extreme cold a bit too much.

- In the 1960s British sci-fi spy thriller TV show, *The Prisoner*, every character had a number for a name. Number 6 was the name of the main character.

- Richard Braine was a British politician with the UK Independence Party (UKIP). His opponents liked to refer to him as "Dick Braine."

- The town of Saint-Louis-du-Ha! Ha! has the dubious distinction of being the only town in the world with two exclamation marks in its name. It's right ahead of Westward Ho!, England.

- A *nom de guerre* ("name of war") is sometimes used by guerillas and terrorists. "Carlos the Jackal" was the *nom de guerre* of Venezuelan terrorist, Ilich Ramírez Sánchez.

- Taumatawhakatangihangakoauauotamateaturipukakapikimaungahoronukupokai-whenuakitanatahu is the longest place name in the world. It's a Māori name for hill in New Zealand, which locals just call "Taumata."

- Harry Baals was the mayor of Fort Wayne, Indiana from 1934 to 1947, and again from 1951 until he died in 1954. His descendants pronounce the name "Bales."

- The nickname "Lefty" is quite popular in the US with lefthanded baseball pitchers, but also some notable gangsters. Mobsters Frank "Lefty" Rosenthal and Benjamin "Lefty" Ruggiero were two notorious lefties.

- Llanfairpwllgwyngyll is the name of a quaint Welsh town on the Island of Anglesey. If you think you've mastered that, try its full name, Llanfair-pwllgwyngyllgogerychwyrndrobwllllantysiliogogogoch.

- Ironic nicknames cross cultures and languages. Men nicknamed "Slim" or "Tiny" are almost always large, as is the case in Spanish-speaking countries with the name "Flaco."

- Pickaway County, Ohio has a number of places named "Hitler," including Hitler Road and Hitler Park. The names come from an influential German American who was not related in any way to *the* Hitler.

- Alfonso IX was the king of the Spanish kingdoms of Leon and Galicia from 1188 to 1230. He played a major role in the Reconquista, but he's best remembered as "The Slobberer."

- Although English-speaking tourists probably giggle when they travel through Condom, France, the French word means "field of the confluence."

- Kash Register is the name of a man who was convicted of murder in 1979 but exonerated in 2013. Register then cashed in when he was awarded $16.7 million for his wrongful conviction.

- If you ever make it to Perry County, Kentucky make sure to drive through Happy Valley before visiting the towns of Happy and Dwarf.

OUT OF THE WATER AND
INTO THE FRYING PAN

○ The whale shark is the largest fish in the world. Whale sharks can grow to 50 feet long and despite the "whale" in its name, it's 100% fish.

○ Chicago Mayor Richard J. Daley gifted 18 bluegills - the Illinois State fish - to the crown prince of Japan in 1960. Once in Japan, the bluegills spread and became an invasive species.

○ Fish breathe oxygen through their gills. The gills diffuse the oxygen through the fish's membranes.

○ The coelacanth is a fish species that was believed to have been extinct for 65 to 66 million years until one was caught off the coast of South Africa in 1938.

There are only two known species of coelacanths: one that lives near the Comoros Islands off the east coast of Africa, and one found in the waters off Sulawesi, Indonesia.

○ The consumption of fish on Fridays during Lent is a Catholic tradition that dates back to the Middle Ages. Interestingly, beaver and alligator were exempted.

○ Every US state has at least one "state fish." Those in the Centrarchidae (sunfish) family are the most popular, which include bass, bluegill, and crappie.

○ The beluga sturgeon is the largest freshwater fish in the world. These beasts can grow to 24 feet long and weigh 2,500 pounds but are only found in the Caspian and the Black Sea basins. The world record was 3,463 lbs. and 23ft 7in long!

○ When the Nubian King Piye conquered Egypt in 728 BCE, he refused to meet with all but one of the chieftains and "kings" of Lower Egyptian because they were "fish eaters."

○ The name Fish Kill or Fishkill actually means the opposite of what you think. "Kill" is derived from the Dutch word for a creek so it means "Fish Creek."

○ A fish's age can be determined by counting rings on its scales or those on its ear bones, which are known as otoliths. These are similar to the rings on trees.

○ "Pan fish" is the term in the US for fish that can fit neatly into a frying pan. Although many species can technically fit the definition, it's generally reserved for sunfish, crappies, and perch.

○ The muskellunge, or "muskie," is the largest member of the freshwater pike family and native to North America. Ferocious predators, muskies have even taken bites out of swimmers!

○ When fish gather for social reasons, such as mating or protection, they are "shoaling." When that group begins moving together in a synchronized way then they are "schooling."

○ In Japanese mythology, Namazu was a giant catfish that lived underground and caused earthquakes. He was especially associated with Lake Biwa.

○ Unlike most fish, which give birth by laying eggs, some shark species - such as hammerheads, bull, and blue sharks - give birth to fully formed "pups."

○ Starfish and jellyfish are not fish. A starfish is an echinoderm, while a jellyfish is cnidaria.

○ "Shore lunches" are popular with recreational fishermen in North America. It simply involves frying any fish you caught that day in a pan over a fire when back on shore or at a camp.

○ Carp includes a number of oily fish species native to Eurasia but considered invasive in most other parts of the world. Goldfish and koi are members of the carp family, Cyprinidae.

○ Except for sharks, most fish don't have eyelids. Fish do, though, have a rest cycle where their brain activity and metabolism are greatly reduced.

○ All fish have vertical tail fins, while aquatic mammals, such as dolphins and whales, have horizontal tail fins. This is probably due to a strange quirk of evolution.

○ The burbot is often referred to as an "eel-pout," but it's actually in the cod family. The burbot is the only freshwater member of the cod family.

○ Seahorses are the only species of fish that swim upright. They're also notable for the male carrying the eggs and giving birth to the brood.

○ Members of the catfish family are "naked" fish without scales. Since catfish don't have scales, they aren't "kosher"!

○ The mudskipper is an amphibious fish that "walks" on its pectoral fins. Because they carry a portable water supply in their gill chambers, mudskippers can survive out of water for long periods.

○ Although live fish often smell like the body they were taken from, freshly cleaned/butchered fish should have almost no odor. A foul odor after cleaning is sign of decay.

TOYS ARE UNIVERSAL

○ Archaeologists have unearthed plenty of ancient Egyptian figurines, but determining which ones were ritual *shabtis* and which were toys/dolls hasn't always been easy. Those found in homes are believed to be toys.

○ When the Pet Rock hit the store shelves in 1975, it became a fad. The fad faded quickly but lasted long enough for creator Gary Dahl to make millions.

○ Sophie la Girafe is a popular teething toy that first came out in France in 1961. It's a cute, seven-inch high rubber giraffe that's become popular around the world.

○ Although the people of Pre-Columbia Mesoamerica never developed wheeled vehicles, they did create what are believed to be wheeled toys for their children.

○ "Stretch Armstrong" was a popular rubber "doll" for boys in the 1970s and '80s that was a bodybuilder you could contort into different shapes. They were filled with blue corn syrup that was often quickly extracted by more curious kids.

○ Rock 'Em Sock 'Em Robots was a game made by Marx that first came out in 1964. The popular game has sold in different versions since the '60s.

○ Hasbro first used the term "action figure" in 1964 to refer to its G.I. Joe figures because they didn't think boys would want a toy called a doll.

○ The ancient Greeks created the world's first mechanical puzzle in the 3rd century BCE. The goal was to create different shapes in a square that was divided into 14 parts.

○ The modern board game Sorry! is basically a rip off of the ancient Indian game, Pachisi. The modern version uses cards instead of shells to determine the movement of pieces.

○ Kongsuni, born in 1969, is the name of a fairly new realistic doll line in South Korea. The doll is so realistic that it "eats" and then farts!

○ *Matryoshka* dolls, or nesting dolls, are those wooden dolls that go inside of each other, progressively getting smaller, or bigger. The first set was made by a Russian craftsman, Vasily Petrovich Zvyozdochkin, in 1890.

○ The Gilbert U-238 Atomic Energy Lab was cool toy that came out in 1950 that was supposed to teach kids about atomic energy. It also came with four uranium ores!

○ The Barbie doll has changed quite a bit since she first came out in 1959. Different versions include 180 careers, 40 nationalities, every race, and thousands of outfits.

○ Marble games have been played for centuries, but in the US and UK, the most popular version is "ringer" (US) or "ring taw" (UK).

○ The Rubik's Cube was invented by Hungarian architect, Ernő Rubik, in 1974. Rubik invented the cube on accident but quickly saw how much fun it could be.

○ Toys "R" Us began life as a single store in New Jersey in 1948 and expanded to nearly every continent before declaring bankruptcy in 2017. A restructured version of the company plans to open new stores.

○ Candy Land requires no skills, strategy, or attention span to play. This is probably what has made Candy Land such a popular board game since 1949.

○ Mattel began cashing in on the "Hot Wheels" line of miniature cars in 1968 and never looked back. The franchise is worth more than $8.5 billion today.

○ In early 2022, the American toy company Hasbro was the largest in the world by market capitalization. Their toys and games include Monopoly and G.I. Joe action figures.

○ You're probably familiar with the stretchy rubbery toy, Play-Doh. Did you know that in 2013 a fecal-centric rip off was released called Poo-Dough? No, it didn't use real poo!

○ When Martin Luther King Junior and Robert Kennedy were assassinated in 1968, Sears Roebuck temporarily removed toy guns from its catalog. They returned to the catalog in 1969.

○ Speaking of marbles, a marble dated to 1900 with the likeness of President Teddy Roosevelt sold for $4,500 on an eBay auction. Now that's a lot of marbles!

○ The wildly popular *Call of Duty* video game franchise came out with action figures in 2004, which included an SS Nazi soldier. The figure was quickly recalled.

○ The "Jolly Chimp" is the common name for the cymbal-banging monkey toy that was popular in the 1960s. Well, it was popular in a creepy way as it's been the subject of more than one horror movie.

○ If you don't include pre-modern games like chess and checkers, Monopoly is the best-selling board game of all time. Since 1935, Monopoly has been released in hundreds of editions.

QUIET ON THE SET

○ The two highest-grossing films of the 1950s were *The Ten Commandments* and *Ben-Hur*. The films helped jumpstart the career of film legend, Charlton Heston.

○ The US has Hollywood, but the UK has Pinewood. Pinewood studios have been the location for many British films and TV shows, including the James Bond franchise.

○ About 70% of all silent films have been lost permanently. Silent films were made with the highly flammable and corrodible chemical, nitrate.

○ Despite the recent popularity of Marvel Universe films, the 2009 film *Avatar* still holds the top spot as the highest-grossing film of all time. *Avatar* has made $2,847,246,203.

○ An "exploitation film" is a movie that attempts to exploit current pop culture trends and usually contains scenes of gratuitous sex, violence, and/or drug use. They were particularly popular in the 1970s.

○ In 1964, only 3% of households in the US had color TV sets. As technology improved, prices went down, so that by 1972 more than 50% of American households had color TV sets.

○ A silver screen is a type of projection screen that was common in the early years of the film industry. The film industry eventually got its nickname from it.

○ The 1980 Italian film, *Cannibal Holocaust*, was one of the first found footage films made. It appeared so real that director Ruggero Deodato was briefly charged with murder.

○ The hit sitcom, *The Honeymooners*, starring Jackie Gleason began as a skit segment on different variety shows before being picked up by CBS. It ran on its own from 1955 through 1956.

- The 1963 film *Cleopatra* cost $44 million to produce, but only took in $40 million in ticket sales, making it one of the first true box office bombs.

- Actor Ken Osmond played Eddie Haskell in the late 1950s-early 1960s American sitcom *Leave it to Beaver*. After the show ended, he was a Los Angeles Police officer for 18 years.

- When the Music Television (MTV) network first aired on August 1, 1981, relatively few people were watching. The first video to play was "Video Killed the Radio Star" by the Buggles.

- The UK's Video Recording Act 1984 stated that VCR tapes for rent or sale had to be classified by the government. This law was the result of exploitation films, which the government called "video nasties," that evaded the censors.

- A TV set would cost $129 to $1,295 in the 1950s. A color set would be at the high end of the scale, easily over $1,000.

- Stan Lee is the highest-grossing actor of all time at $30,607,168,726, but that includes cameos and voice acting. Samuel Jackson is second with $27,684,734,363.

- *The Simpsons* have broken many records in American television. For the number of seasons and episodes, it is the longest-running animated series, longest-running sitcom, and the longest-running scripted primetime television series.

- Thomas Edison was influential in the early film industry. He invented a motion picture viewer called the kinetoscope and started film studios in New Jersey and New York.

- The 1914 British film, *The World, the Flesh and the Devil* is the first feature-length, fictional film in color. The silent film has unfortunately been lost (see above comment on the loss of silent films).

- The series finale of *M*A*S*H*, which aired on February 28, 1983, was watched by more than 60% of all American households. It's still the most-watched TV episode in history.

- The highest-grossing silent film of all time is D.W's Griffith's 1915 *Birth of a Nation*. It may seem crazy that the Ku Klux Klan were actually the good guys in that film!

- After the 1970-71 TV season, American TV executives collectively cancelled nearly all of the Western and other rural-themed shows in what became known as the "rural purge."

○ When *Star Wars* came out in 1977, it was different in many ways from anything before it. One notable trend it started was merchandizing, from action figures to clothing.

○ The most expensive Bollywood film of all time was the science fiction movie *Ra One* (2011). It cost $35 million to make.

○ Throughout the 1940s, many TV shows had a 15-minute, instead of a 30- or 60-minute format. Most networks also only broadcast for a few hours a day.

○ *Gunsmoke* produced more episodes than any other live-action American TV show with 635 episodes. *Law and Order: Special Victims Unit*, which is still airing, is second with 512 episodes.

GARBAGE IS A SERIOUS BUSINESS

○ WASH is an acronym for "water, sanitation, and hygiene." It was developed by the World Health Organization (WHO) to identify regions lacking basic services.

○ "Waste management" is a euphemism that refers to the collection, treatment, and disposal of waste (garbage). "Municipal solid waste" refers to food and other garbage that's collected and disposed of.

○ Americans generally call it "garbage" or "trash," but the British call it "rubbish." The Australians can call it any of those depending on the situation.

○ The Romans were the first people to build an extensive sewer system. The Cloaca Maxima was the name of the sewer system that ran under Rome and was built in the 6th century BCE.

- About 54% of the world's population had access to proper sanitation services in 2020, but that left more than 1.7 billion people without private toilets.

- In 2016, 33% of all solid waste in the world was disposed of in open dumps, while landfills comprise just over 25%. Recycling was number three at 13.5%.

- Waste Management Inc. was the leading American waste management company in 2021 with $14.5 billion in revenue and 42,300 employees. Trash is sure gold for this company.

- President James Garfield was shot on July 2, 1881 but lingered for weeks before dying on September 19. The bullet was the catalyst in the assassination, but dirty hands and instruments played a role in his ultimate demise.

- The omni processor is a machine that removes pathogens from poop. Bill Gates believes in it so much he drank a glass of water that came from one.

- Modern sanitation in all countries generally follows the same process. Waste is first contained and then emptied by a sanitation company or municipal authorities. It's then transported and treated where it is then either disposed of or recycled.

- The diseases and afflictions that poor sanitation can lead to include diarrheal derived diseases such as cholera and dysentery. Typhoid, intestinal worms, and even polio are some of the diseases, also possible.

- Organized crime has been involved in the sanitation business in many parts of the world. Experts cite the ease to enter the profession and profits that can be made as among the reasons.

- Englishman Thomas Crapper (1836-1910) didn't invent the toilet, but he did improve plumbing by inventing the "U-bend" trap. It prevents liquids and gasses from flowing back into the toilet. The actual invention of the flush toilet can be traced back to a British man named Sir John Harrington who, in 1596, devised a mechanism with a cord that, when pulled, flushed away waste with a rush of water.

- The Apex Regional landfill in Las Vegas, Nevada is the largest landfill in the world. Its trash sprawls over 2,200 acres and receives more than 9,000 tons daily.

- Before the Romans, the people of the Indus Valley Civilization (3,300-1,300 BCE) disposed of sewage through underground drains. They weren't as complex as what the Romans built, but they were the first in the world.

- The average person will spend about one to one and a half years on the toilet in a lifetime. Men spend more time on the throne than women.

- About 494 million people still do their business in public. This number includes those with no other options, not those walking home from the bar on a Saturday night.

- If you're an American or Canadian visiting Europe for the first time, that thing next to the toilet isn't a urinal, it's a *bidet*. Bidets, similar to a toilet bowl but shorter in height, are typically used to wash off intimate areas after using the toilet.

- Landfills produce large amounts of methane gas. Properly managed landfills gather the methane emissions to produce electricity, heat, and fuel.

- "Garbology" is the study of garbage and sanitation. Developed by Dr. William Rathje at the University of Arizona in 1973, it's a multi-discipline study that involves archeology, history, and sociology.

- Jain monks are forbidden from washing any parts of their bodies except their hands and feet. Bathing kills microorganisms, which is against the creed of Jain monks.

- The world's first true toothbrush was invented in China during the Tang Dynasty (619-907). The bristles were made from hog hairs, which doesn't scream "sanitary," does it?

- Septic tanks are common forms of sanitation in rural regions of the industrialized world. They're examples of onsite sewage facilities (ossf).

- "Puerperal fever" refers to bacterial infections acquired during childbirth, usually due to unclean doctors or nurses. These infections are the cause of about 10% of all deaths after pregnancy.

- When condoms, maxi pads, and other non-biodegradable solids are flushed down toilets, they can combine with grease and form "fatbergs," which are as hard as rocks.

THE WORLD OF MICROCELEBRITIES

○ A microcelebrity is someone who gained fame on the internet. Due to the nature of their fame, they are sometimes referred to as "eCelebs."

○ Video sharing and social media site 'YouTube' launched on February 14, 2005. It's since become the main platform for microcelebrities, who are also known as "YouTubers."

○ Many microcelebrities court controversy to increase clicks. On December 31, 2017, Logan Paul uploaded a video to his YouTube video of a suicide victim in the Aokigahara of Japan. Paul was temporarily removed from YouTube.

○ "Viral videos" have made many people famous in the internet era, but they've been around for some time. The TV show *Candid Camera* is an early example.

○ The late Kimbo Slice got his start by uploading his street fights to the internet. The website became popular, allowing him to segue into a semi-successful MMA career.

○ "Content creation" refers to the process of creating something for the internet. The definition can fit many things, but since it fits all microcelebrities, they are often called "content creators."

○ "Monetization," whereby YouTube creators charge subscription fees for their channels, began in 2013. In 2018, the monetization rules were changed to require 1,000 subscribers who watch at least 4,000 hours of content.

○ Chinese social networking site, TikTok, launched in 2017 and has since become popular with younger content creators who focus on video editing.

○ Swedish YouTuber PewDiePie (Felix Arvid Ulf Kjellberg) currently has the fourth-most subscriptions to his YouTube channel with over 111 million. The channel was primarily gaming orientated at first but evolved into comedy.

○ Jake Paul is the younger brother of Logan Paul. Although Jake has had a successful acting and content creation career, he's more recently fought as a professional boxer.

- The social media site for beautiful people, Instagram, was launched in 2010. It was acquired by Facebook in 2012 for $1 billion.

- North Korea blocks access to YouTube, Instagram, and TikTok. In fact, North Korea blocks access to most of the world wide web and only allows access to government workers.

- The band, Sons of Maxwell, made the video "United Breaks Guitars" for their YouTube channel to protest the destruction of one of their instruments, but it made them famous, temporarily.

- Patreon is another site frequently used by content creators. Fans can pay reoccurring charges or per specific releases of content.

- Indian-based YouTube channel, T-Series, tops all others with 213 million subscriptions. T-Series began in 1983 by pirating pirated Bollywood music but became a music label in the 1990s.

- Sam Hyde is a controversial comedian from Rhode Island who's best known for pulling pranks and trolls and posting them online. He's also been mistakenly associated with mass shootings.

- Although TikTok is a Chinese company, the Chinese government blocks the overseas version, tiktok.com, on the mainland.

- Plenty of women have made lots of money and gained lots of fame selling subscriptions to their Only Fans channels. The London-based company planned to ban porn and adult content in 2021, but after backlash from content creators, the decision was reversed six days later.

- YouTube acknowledged the importance of its content creators on June 28, 2012, through the YouTube Creator Awards. Awards are given based on the number of subscribers: Silver, Gold, Diamond, Custom, and Red Diamond.

- American teenager Charli D'Amelio has the most followers on TikTok with 139.4 million and has a net worth of approximately $12 million. Her older sister, Dixie, is tenth with 57.8 million followers.

- Mr. Beast (Jimmy Donaldson) has collected millions of clicks on his YouTube channel for his stunt and survival challenges. He's also known for donating much of his profits to charity. He has a net worth of approximately $25 million.

- Iran blocks most social media internet sites, including those popular with content creators, such as YouTube, Snapchat, and Only Fans. Somewhat surprising, though, Instagram is not blocked.

○ After Western countries placed sanctions on Russia for its February 2022 invasion of Ukraine, Russia responded by blocking Instagram and some other Western-based social media sites.

○ In 2011, American teenager Rebecca Black's life changed when her low-budget YouTube video-son, "Friday," was released. A month after it was uploaded, it had one million views, launching Black's career.

○ Feuds between content creators are common. In 2017, creators iDubbbz and RiceGum released hip hop "diss tracks" against each other. iDubbbz also released a video for the song, "Asian Jake Paul," that has more than 85 million views.

DO YOU THINK POLYESTER WILL MAKE A COMEBACK?

○ The earliest evidence of human clothing comes from Morocco and is dated between 120,000 to 90,000 years ago. Some scholars believe some clothing may even be older.

○ A textile is any flexible material that is made by combining threads. Textiles can be made from natural or synthetic materials, and natural materials can come from plants or animals.

○ Many people believe that all polyesters are synthetic, but many actually include naturally occurring chemicals. Polyesters are defined as polymer materials that contain a specific chemical compound known as ester.

○ Cotton is the most commonly used natural fiber in clothing throughout the world. Polyester is the most produced synthetic fiber and the most used fiber overall, so polyester never really went away!

○ The 1980s had many unique styles that may or may not make a comeback. Velcro straps in place of shoelaces are still yet to make a reappearance.

○ Linen is a textile made from the flax plant. It was commonly used for clothing in the ancient world in Mesopotamia, Egypt, and the Levant.

○ Nearly two million people in the US are employed in the fashion industry. Interestingly, 340,000 are employed in fashion in Germany and France but 550,000 work in fashion in the UK.

○ The first silk road era began in the late 2nd century BCE and lasted until the mid-3rd century CE. The primary states were Han China, Parthian Persia, Rome, and the Kushan Empire.

○ During the Weimar Period of German history (the 1920s), Berlin rivaled Paris and New York as a premier fashion capital.

○ Buttons are always on the right side of men's shirts, while they're on the left for women. The reason for this isn't clear.

○ That tiny extra front pocket on your jeans was used to hold pocket watches. When the first Levi jeans were sold in 1879, most men carried pocket watches.

○ The average American throws out about 82 pounds of textiles per year. Those clothes usually end up in landfills, where an article of clothing can take 40 years to decompose.

○ Spanish company Inditex was the world's largest clothing retailer in sales with $28.89 billion in revenue. Zara is its flagship store.

○ The earliest wool textiles in Europe date to about 1,500 BCE, but it wasn't until the early Middle Ages (400s-1100s CE) that wool became a popular material for clothing.

○ A survey revealed that the average woman hasn't worn $550 worth of clothing they own or about 20% of their wardrobe. Interestingly, shoes are the number one unworn item.

○ The turban has been a traditional headwear in the Middle East and South Asia for centuries. In the 1800s, though, the cylindrical shaped hat with the tassel known as the fez became popular in the Ottoman Empire.

○ In the US, a haberdasher is a retailer who sells men's clothing. A haberdashery is a location where the clothing is sold and may employ a tailor for custom fittings.

○ On average, Americans spend about 3.5% of their income on clothes. This may seem like a lot, but it's down quite a bit from the 11.5% of the 1950s.

○ In 2021, North Korean dictator, Kim Jong-un, banned skinny jeans, mullets, and branded t-shirts to stop foreign influence. The mullet thing was probably a good move, but his own haircut is a little strange?

○ A "fashion house" is a company that makes high-end fashion. Charles Frederick Worth (1825-1895) started the idea in the late 1800s when he sewed his label onto his finished products.

○ The "YKK" you see on most zippers stands for *Yoshida Kōgyō Kabushiki gaisha* (YKK Group), which is the largest zipper manufacturer in the world.

○ China is currently the world's largest producer and exporter of textiles. It has an export value of about $266.41 billion.

○ Although most clothing material is recyclable, only 15% of people recycle their old clothing. Also, only about 1% of the material used to make clothing is later recycled.

❍ Trousers first gained widespread use in the 6th century BCE in Central Asia among the nomadic peoples of the steppe. The Greeks and Romans viewed trousers as barbaric.

❍ South Korean President Park Chung-hee took fashion seriously when he was in charge from 1963 to 1979. Under his rule, police checked the lengths of women's skirts to make sure they weren't too short!

FOR ALL YOU CAT LOVERS

○ A cat's best sense is its hearing. They can rotate their ears 180 degrees and are capable of hearing 1.6 octaves above the range of a human and 1 octave above that of a dog.

○ A Calico is not a breed; it's any tri-color coat domestic cat. Calico cats are almost always female.

○ Cats have better night vision than humans, but they are nearsighted. A cat's visual acuity ranges from 20/100 to 20/200.

○ The ancient Egyptians revered cats in different forms. Bastet was the peaceful domestic cat goddess who guarded the home, while Sekhmet was the ferocious lioness goddess of war.

- Since cats rarely "meow" toward each other, and only seem to do so toward humans, experts believe it's a trait they developed after domestication.

- Cats groom each other by licking to be social, which is known as allogrooming. If your cat happens to lick you, it just means she's accepted you into the group.

- The Maine coon is the largest cat breed in the world. These shaggy kitties can grow to a length of 38 inches and males can weigh up to 18 pounds.

- Dogs may be man's best friend, but there are more than 73 million cats in North America compared to 63 million dogs.

- A dog's brain is larger than a cat's, but a cat's brain is more complex. Cat brains have about 300 million neurons compared to about 160 million for dogs.

- Crème Puff the cat was born on August 3, 1967, and passed away on August 5, 2005, at the age of 38, making her the oldest cat on record. She had only one owner, Jake Perry.

- The ancient Egyptians mummified sacred animals, such as cats. Thousands of cat mummies were dedicated to Bubastis in a section of the sacred animal necropolis of Saqqara known as the Bubasteion.

- It's commonly believed that one human year equals seven cat years. Vets, though, multiply the cat's year by four and add 16 years to get the "cat years."

- The Greeks and Romans preferred to keep weasels for rodent control. With that said, they did admire feline intelligence and independence.

- Cats sleep from 12 to 20 hours a day. Although cats are usually light sleepers, they enter periods of rapid eye movement and likely dream.

- If you own a bunch of cats, then you have a clowder on your hands. The term "clowder" is only used to describe groups of domestic cats.

- The CIA's Directorate of Science and Technology's Operation Acoustic Kitty was a plan was to implant listening devices in cats in the 1960s. Not surprising, the program was shut down in 1967.

- If you go to Guangdong in China and order "dragon, tiger, phoenix," you'll get a plate of specially cooked cat, snake, and chicken! It's believed to give strength. Good luck with the meal.

- Although cats do love milk, and it's not inherently toxic for them, most cats are actually lactose intolerant.

- The ancient Egyptian word for a cat was the onomatopoetic, *mieu*. This was similar to how their name for "dog" (see above).

- The reputation of black cats has evolved through history. Early European cultures saw them as clever and fortuitous, but by the Middle Ages, they became associated with witchcraft.

- Kopi luwak is a rare and usually expensive coffee from Indonesia. One of the ingredients is coffee cherries that have been eaten and pooped out by a wild cat (Asian palm civet.)

- The original "Morris the Cat," the spokescat for the 9Lives brand of cat food, was discovered at a Chicago animal shelter in 1968.

- A cat usually has 24 whiskers, 12 on each side. Whiskers help cats navigate and determine distance, although they technically don't help them "see" any better.

- Although the Sphynx breed of cat may have an ancient name, they're relatively new. Sphynxes were created through selective breeding in 1966 in Toronto, Ontario.

- Islam has traditionally viewed dogs as "unclean," so they aren't very common as pets in the Middle East. Cats were kept by Mohammad and considered "clean."

POP STAR TRAGEDIES

○ An early tragedy Michael Jackson suffered was when his hair caught on fire while shooting a Pepsi commercial on January 27, 1984, in Los Angeles. Jokes were made about the incident, but it left Jackson scarred and addicted to painkillers.

○ Ricky Nelson was a '50s teen idol who was still well-known in the 1980s. Nelson died when the small DC-3 he was on crashed on December 31, 1985.

○ "The Day the Music Died" refers to February 3, 1959, regarding an airplane crash in Iowa that took the lives of rockers Buddy Holly, the Big Bopper, and Richie Valens.

○ On December 8, 1980, former Beatle singer John Lennon was shot and killed by Mark David Chapman in New York City. At his sentencing, Chapman read an excerpt from *The Catcher in the Rye*.

○ Sergio Gomez was a star in Mexico's Duranguense music scene. After playing a show on December 2, 2007, Gomez was abducted, tortured, and murdered. No one has ever been arrested.

○ Many K-Pop stars have died at young ages, several in auto accidents. Two members of the band Ladies' Code - RiSe and EunB - died from injuries from the same September 3, 2014, car crash.

○ Several legends and rumors surround the death of Jimi Hendrix. The official report stated that he choked on his vomit, but the accounts given by the last person to see him alive, Monika Dannemann, reportedly changed the view, but Asphyxia due to aspiration of vomit; contributed to by barbiturate intoxication is still stated as the cause.

○ You may remember Blind Melon's hit "No Rain" and then forgot about them. Part of that is because lead singer, Shannon Hoon, died of a cocaine overdose on October 21, 1995.

- Kurt Cobain's April 5, 1994, suicide was/is thought by some people to be a murder cover-up. Some conspiracy theories were even considered on an episode of *Unsolved Mysteries*.

- Ellen Naomi Cohen, better known as "Cass Elliot" or "Mama Cass," struggled with her weight her entire, short life. She died of a heart attack on July 29, 1974, at the age of 32.

- Patsy Cline was only 30 and taking over the country music world when she died in a plane crash on March 5, 1963, near Camden, Tennessee.

- On August 10, 1993, Norwegian black metal musician, Varg Vikernes, stabbed former friend and fellow musician, Øystein Aarseth to death, bringing global media attention to the Scandinavian metal scene.

- The Mexican American pop star, Selena Quintanilla Pérez, was set to cross over from Latin music to mainstream pop when she was shot and killed by Yolanda Saldívar on March 31, 1995.

- Rapper Eazy-E (Eric Lynn Wright) became one of the first, and highest-profile, pop stars to die of AIDs on March 26, 1995.

- Suicide is also fairly common in the high-pressure world of K-Pop. On October 14, 2019, pop star Sulli hanged herself to death and just over a month later, on November 24, star Goo Hara committed suicide.

- People know the 1973 song "Bad, Bad Leroy Brown," but not its singer. The reason is that singer Jim Croce died in a plane crash on September 20, 1973.

- Elvis Presley died on August 16, 1977, at the age of 42 of a heart attack. It was determined that obesity and heavy drug use played contributing roles.

- The murder of rapper Tupac Shakur on September 13, 1996 was once thought to be part of a conspiracy, but the evidence shows it was likely a local beef.

- Swedish DJ, Avicii (Tim Bergling), committed suicide while on vacation in Oman in 2018. He had struggled with opioid and alcohol addiction for several years.

- The "27 Club" is an urban myth that pop stars are more likely to die at that age than any other. Recent studies have shown that this isn't true.

- Rapper Notorious B.I.G. (Christopher Wallace) was gunned down in LA on March 9, 1997. Many believed it was retaliation for Tupac's murder, by Wardell Fouse, but Fouse was murdered in 2003 so we'll probably never know.

- Judy Garland was the original tragic pop star. She died of a barbiturate overdose, on June 22, 1969, at the age of 47.

- Jim Morrison could've been *the* rockstar of the 1970s, or a prize-winning poet, but instead, he overdosed on heroin in a bathroom of a Paris hotel on July 3, 1971.

- Jaco Pastorius was a promising jazz musician with a drug problem and a tendency to start bar fights. On September 21, 1987, he started a fight with a martial arts expert at a bar and was beaten to death.

- Musicians in the above mentioned "27 Club" include Jimi Hendrix, Jim Morrison, Brian Jones, Janis Joplin, Kurt Cobain, and Amy Winehouse.

KEEPING TIME

○ "Time" has been defined as the sequence of existence into a series or sequence of events that can't be reversed. With that said, some scientific theories argue it's possible to change the sequencing.

○ Water clocks were the most reliable early clocks. The oldest examples of water clocks come from 16th century BCE Egypt and Mesopotamia.

○ The "grandfather paradox" holds that if a time traveler were able to go back in time and kill their grandfather then the time traveler wouldn't be born. But if the time traveler wasn't born, then they couldn't go back to kill grandpa, right?

○ Following the course of the moon and sun were the earliest, most reliable forms of timekeeping. For that reason, calendars were developed before clocks.

○ "Coordinated Universal Time" UTC is the standard by which all time is regulated. All time zones on Earth are based on the system, ranging from -12:00 UTC to +14:00 UTC.

○ The academic term for a "leap year" is an intercalary year. This happens because a true solar year is slightly more than 365 days.

○ The world's oldest sundial dates to about 1,500 BCE in Egypt. But telling time from shadows was the earliest type of timekeeping.

○ It takes just under 24 hours for the Earth to rotate. The precise time is 23 hours, 56 minutes, and four seconds.

○ There are actually measures of time less than a second. A Planck time is the period it takes light to travel one Planck in a vacuum or 5.39×10^{-44} seconds.

○ In 2018, a lag in the European power grid caused the clocks on the continent to be six minutes slow. The problem was resolved after a few months.

○ The first mechanical clocks began appearing in Western Europe in the late 1200s. The earliest clockmakers were German, with the German and Swiss clockmaking tradition continuing to the present.

- "Greenwich Mean Time" GMT, refers to the time at the Royal Observatory in Greenwich, England. Although it's commonly thought to be synonymous with UTC, it's actually the time zone UTC +0:00.

- Rolex was actually founded in London, England in 1905 but moved its headquarters to the watch/clock capital of Geneva, Switzerland in 1920, where it remains today.

- The Greek word for water clock is *clepsydra*. Water clocks worked simply by either filling a vessel and draining it slowly and evenly or filling it slowly and evenly.

- Julius Caesar employed the brightest thinkers in the Roman Republic to create a new calendar that solved the problem of leap year. The Julian Calendar went into effect on January 1, 45 BCE and lasted until CE 1582 in most Western countries.

- Purely lunar calendars were rare in the pre-modern world. Lunisolar calendars base their months on the Moon's cycles but account for leap years to stay in agreement with the solar calendar.

- An atomic clock keeps time by determining the frequency of the radiation of atoms. Atomic clocks were developed in the 1950s for commercial use.

- Cuckoo clocks originated in the mid-1700s in Germany. They came a little after the grandfather clock, which was invented by English clockmaker William Clement in 1670.

- Due to the intercalary days on the calendar, the Egyptian civil calendar only synchronized with the genuine seasonal years once every 1,460 years.

- The Doomsday Clock is a symbolic clock that was devised in 1949 by the *Bulletin of Atomic Scientists* to predict how close the Earth is to doomsday, with midnight being doomsday. As of 2022, the clock is at 100 seconds to midnight, the closest it has ever been.

- Back in the 1980s, everyone had to have a Swatch watch. Swatch was a new Swiss watch company at the time, founded in 1983.

- The Gregorian calendar was introduced in 1582 by Pope Gregory XIII. The leap years were spaced differently in the Gregorian calendar to correspond with the 365.2422 days of the true solar year.

- "Flip clocks" are electromechanical digital clocks that were popular in the 1970s. Those who collect or repair these obsolete devices are known as horopalettologists.

○ From 1700 to 1712, Sweden used its own calendar, which resulted in a February 30 in 1712. Sweden went back to the Julian calendar in 1712.

○ If you're an American and planning a trip to Europe, keep in mind that most European countries use 24-hour time. In fact, most of the world uses 24-hour time officially.

METEOROLOGICAL MADNESS

- ○ Meteorology is a branch of Earth sciences that focuses on weather forecasting. It's been around for centuries, but it only took its modern, scientific look in the 1700s.

- ○ The Medieval Warm Period (MWP) was a period of warming in the North Atlantic from about CE 950 to 1250. The warming allowed the Vikings to build settlements in Greenland which were subsequently abandoned due to climate conditions changing.

- ○ Mawsynram, India holds the Guinness World Record for the most rainfall in a single year, with 1,000 inches in 1985. The village averages 467 inches of rain per year.

- Today, most television news weather presenters in the US have degrees in meteorology, but back in the 1960s, they were usually "weather girls" who were known more for their looks than their knowledge.

- The Weather Channel (TWC) began airing on May 2, 1982. The channel was rated as the most trusted media network in a 2022 *Economist* poll.

- A hurricane is a storm system that rapidly rotates and is marked by a low-pressure center, or "eye." In most locations, these are known as cyclones, but in the North Atlantic and Eastern Pacific, they are hurricanes.

- About 2,000 people are killed by lightning strikes every year. Florida leads the US in deaths by lightning, with about ten killed each year.

- Mount Washington in New Hampshire holds the record for the fastest recorded wind gust on the land at 231 mph in 1934. It held the overall mark until higher gusts off the coast of Barrow Island, Australia were recorded in 1996.

- Meteorologists use many tools to predict the weather, including satellite technology. Doppler weather radar has been used since the 1960s, with weather radar networks forming in the 1980s.

- The Maya storm god was named *Huracan*, which may be the origin of the word "Hurricane," although some believe it was derived from the name of a Taino god.

- The Russian research station, Vostok Station, in Antarctica is the site of the lowest recorded temperature on Earth. On July 21, 1983, the lonely station hit -128.6 °F.

- Hurricanes/cyclones spin counterclockwise in the northern hemisphere, but cyclones in the southern hemisphere spin clockwise. This because in the southern hemisphere, winds traveling toward the equator will move eastward, and winds traveling toward the South Pole will curve west, which is known as the Coriolis effect.

- The largest piece of hail recorded was found in Vivian, South Dakota on July 23, 2010. It weighed nearly two pounds and was eight inches in diameter.

- First published in 1818, the *Farmers' Almanac* was one of the first publications to make meteorological predictions. Despite skeptics, the *Almanac* retains a loyal following.

- The Armistice Day Blizzard of 1940 left 154 people dead across the Upper Midwest, making it one of the worst snowstorms in American history.

- Like a hurricane, a tornado is a rapidly rotating storm with a low-pressure center. It also rotates clockwise or counterclockwise depending on which hemisphere it is located in.

- The highest recorded temperature on Earth was 134 °F. It was recorded on July 10, 1913, at Furnace Creek, California, in Death Valley, on July 10, 1913.

- The "Little Ice Age" refers to the climatic period after the Medieval Warm Period, from the 1500s through the 1800s when the Earth cooled as much as 3.6 °F.

- If you've ever hiked high in the Sierra Nevada Mountains, you may have noticed pink snow. It's that color because of a type of algae called chlamydomonas nivalis that thrives in cold environments.

- The US experiences more tornadoes than any other country, with about 1,200 per year. Within the US, more tornadoes happen in the Plains states, which are known as "Tornado Alley."

- Chicago isn't even in the top ten windiest cities in America. Mount Washington, New Hampshire (see above), tops the list, followed by Dodge City, Kansas.

- The 2009 Australian Dust Storm began in the Australian Outback on September 22 and then quickly moved east for two days, picking up sand along the way and shutting down Sydney.

- Florida actually has the highest number of tornados per capita in the US, but they are often weaker "waterspout" tornados.

- It's estimated that about 22 million tons of salt are used on US roads every winter. As tough as that salt is on cars, it saves many lives but pollutes the landscape.

- The city of Aomori, Japan, located on the northern tip of the main island, holds the record for the heaviest annual snowfall in the world at 57.87 feet.

TILL DEATH DO US PART

○ As of 2019, one in three marriages were considered "low sex" or "no sex." I guess that's why my married friends envy my single status!

○ Marriage ceremonies were generally absent in the ancient world. Two families would often arrange a coupling and the couple would then cohabitate, constituting a marriage.

○ Most English-speaking countries began allowing "no-fault divorces" in the early 1970s. California was the first US state to allow no-fault divorce in 1970.

○ The origins of throwing rice at a wedding are disputed, but it's believed by many to have started with Romans throwing wheat at new couples. The tradition eventually evolved to rice.

○ The Unification Church, also known as the Moonies, has promoted arranged marriages where couples are wed in mass events. A 1982 mass wedding at Madison Square Garden in New York wed 2,075 couples.

○ The Greek Ptolemy dynasty that ruled Egypt after Alexander the Great regularly practiced consanguineous marriage (that is, marriage to people descended from the same ancestor). Cleopatra was married to two of her brothers, Ptolemy XIII and Ptolemy XIV.

○ Herbert and Zelmyra Fisher were married for a world record 86 years before Herbert passed away in 2011 at the age of 106.

○ The tradition of wedding cakes probably originated in ancient Rome, where the bride would have bread broken over her head for luck.

○ The dowry is the price the groom's family has to pay for the bride. Once common throughout the world, they are still part of many marriages in parts of Asia, Africa, and the Middle East.

○ The Bible belt doesn't seem to slow divorce. Arkansas and Oklahoma have the highest rate of people who have been married at least three times.

- Don't do it! Studies show that 75% of all marriages that start with an affair end in divorce. That's considerably higher than the average divorce rate.

- Men in ancient Greece were expected to marry and have families, but they also often took young male lovers.

- The average length of a marriage in the US is 11 years. Although the overall divorce rates have declined since their 1981 peak, about 45% of marriages still end in divorce.

- Slaves in the US south weren't allowed to legally marry, but they still did. The American slave wedding ceremony involved the betrothed jumping over a broom to seal the deal!

- According to the *Guinness Book of World Records*, Bertie and Jessie Wood are the oldest couple to divorce. They were both 98 when they ended their 36-year marriage.

- White wedding dresses didn't become common until Queen Victoria married in 1840. She also started the style of the modern wedding ceremony, which became known as a "white wedding."

- Polygamy has generally been frowned upon or outlawed in most Western societies throughout history. The notable exception is the Church of Jesus Christ of Latter-day Saints (Mormons), although the Church officially banned the practice in 1890.

- The 1955 song "Love and Marriage" by Frank Sinatra became a hit on the radio charts and was later used as the theme song for the hit '90s sitcom, *Married... with Children*.

- Members of the Amish community are only allowed to marry once they are baptized and become full members of the church. Courting usually begins when they're in their teens.

- There are numerous written records of divorce in ancient Egypt. It should be noted that most "marriage contracts" from ancient Egypt, date to the Late and Ptolemaic periods (747-30 BCE).

- Elopement is common enough that it has its own word in different languages. In the Philippines, it's called *tanan*, while in Indonesia and Malaysia it's known as *kahwin lari*.

- Polyandry is a type of polygamy where a woman takes more than one husband at a time. It's historically much rarer than polygyny (a man having multiple wives) and has rarely enjoyed institutional support.

- If you thought Liz Taylor and her seven failed marriages was bad, she had nothing on Linda Wolfe. Wolfe has the world record for the woman with the most marriages, having married 23 times, although three of those marriages were to the same man.

- Charivari was a post-wedding ceremony that was once popular in Europe and North America. It involved a group doing a parade and a mock serenade of the newlyweds, often in protest of the union.

- The global wedding industry was worth over $300 billion in 2016 and over $60 billion in the US alone. I guess all those divorces are paying off for someone!

INCREDIBLE CRIME FACTS

- In 2016, Chastity Eugina Hopson "learned" on social media that meth and heroin could be contaminated with the Ebola strain. So, she did the responsible thing and gave her stash to the police.

- Jeffrey Dahmer's neighbors in his Milwaukee apartment building said he was a really nice and quiet guy. He even occasionally gave his neighbors some "homemade" sandwiches.

- In a fictional "crime caper" story, the reader or viewer knows the identity of the criminal, with the focus being on the "heist." Capers are generally lighter and less violent than a straight crime story.

- Contrary to common media portrayals, most burglaries take place between 10 a.m. and 3 p.m. Professional crooks strike when homeowners are at work or school.

- Nearly every royal tomb from ancient Egypt's New Kingdom (ca. 1,550-1,075 BCE) was plundered. In most cases, it was the original tomb builders who took everything.

- Studies show that only about half of all serious violent crimes in the US - which include rape, robbery, and aggravated assault - are reported.

- The "Florida Man" internet meme - where strange crimes committed by men from Florida are humorously showcased - became popular in 2013. It then made a comeback in 2020.

- On March 18, 1990, thieves made off with 13 works of art from the Isabella Stewart Gardner Museum in Boston, Massachusetts valued at $600 million by the late 2000s. No arrests have been made, although known mobsters are suspected.

- Most of the world's most industrialized nations have abolished execution as the top criminal punishment. The US, Japan, and Singapore are three notable exceptions.

- In 2010, a Florida crew of five criminals led by Jose David Diaz-Marrero stole some vases that contained what they believed were crushed up pills. After snorting the substance, they later learned it was the ashes of a man and two great Danes.

- The Romans built the Mamertine Prison in the 7th century BCE as a place of temporary detention. The Christian saints' Peter and Paul were held there.

- Necrophilia is punishable by death in the Philippines, but due to legal loopholes, it's technically legal in many US states.

- Mohammad Ashan was a Taliban terrorist with $100 on his head. In 2012, Ashan attempted to turn himself in to get the reward but was arrested instead.

- According to the FBI, Anchorage, Alaska ranked second among US cities in crime rate. The cold weather apparently doesn't keep the criminals in check.

- From 1986 to 2013, Christopher Thomas Knight (born 1965) lived as a hermit in rural Maine. He burglarized homes and camps occasionally, which is how he was eventually caught.

- Mexico comes in at a moderately safe 44th overall in terms of crime rate. But in 2019, the five cities with the highest homicide rates were all in Mexico.

- Ancient Egyptian criminals could be lashed or even have their nose and ears amputated before being sent to work in a granite quarry. Tomb robbers were often impaled.

- Studies have shown that in the 1700s, 80% of male pickpockets operated in public settings, while 78% of female pickpockets, who were often prostitutes, worked in private locations.

- From 2015 to 2017, the tiny nation of Luxembourg led the EU in car thefts per capita. The country's wealth is likely a draw for opportunistic European criminals.

- If you ever spend time in Saudi Arabia, remember to keep your head! Beheading by scimitar is the punishment for crimes including blasphemy and apostasy.

- When James Blankenship was arrested for breaking into his mother's home in June 2013, he thought he was in the clear, not because it was his mom's house but because he thought you could only be charged for burglaries that happen at night!

- The top honor for the country with the highest crime rate currently goes to Venezuela. The US is 57th, but plenty of its cities are among the most dangerous.

- Although law codes preceded the Law Code of Hammurabi (1,755–1,750 BCE), the Babylonian code was the most detailed and complete to that point. The concept of swift and harsh punishment was laid out in the Code.

- In 2019, Tijuana, Mexico had the world's highest homicide rate, but Cape Town, South Africa had the most murders, with 3,065.

- China isn't afraid to execute its billionaires. In 2006, tycoon Yuan Baojing was executed for ordering murder contracts on his rivals, including Liu Han, who was himself executed in 2015.

WARRIOR WOMEN

○ "Molly Pitcher" is the legendary name of either Mary Ludwig Hays McCauley or Margaret Hays. The story is that "Molly" carried pitchers of water to Patriot troops to cool the canons during a battle in the American Revolution.

○ Hanna Reitsch was a German aviator who was a test pilot for the Luftwaffe during World War II. She flew the last Luftwaffe plane out of Berlin in 1945.

○ The Nigerian Islamist terrorist group, Boko Haram, is the first organization to use women in a majority of its suicide bombings.

○ Deborah Sampson Gannett fought in combat for the Patriots during the American Revolution under the name Robert Shirtliff. When her gender was revealed, Gannett was given an honorable discharge.

- North Korea practices "selective conscription" for women, which means if a woman has the skills the military needs, then she really has no choice but to join.

- In Greek mythology, the Amazons were a society of all-female warriors and hunters. They only had relations with men to produce female offspring; boys were either killed or returned to their fathers.

- Israel requires women as well as men to serve in its military and is one of the few militaries where women serve in combat roles.

- WAVES is an acronym that stands for Women Accepted for Volunteer Emergency Service. This was a branch of the US Navy Reserve where women served as officers in non-combat roles during World War II.

- Major Margaret J. "Hot Lips" Houlihan is one of the best known fictional military women. She was a nurse with the rank of major in the *M*A*S*H* franchise.

- Norway and Israel both began allowing women in all military units in 1985. Norway became the first NATO country to do so.

- Warrior goddesses were not uncommon in the ancient world. The Greek goddess Athena, the Assyrian goddess Ishtar, and the Egyptian lioness headed goddess Sekhmet, were all martial deities.

- "Apache" was the name of a mysterious female sniper who fought for the Viet Cong during the Vietnam War. She was killed in 1966 by American sniper, Carlos Hathcock.

- During World War II, more than 1,000 female snipers fought for the Red Army. A regiment of female fighter pilots also took on the Luftwaffe.

- Boudica known in Latin chronicles as Boadicea or Boudicea, and in Welsh as Buddug, was a queen of the British Iceni tribe who led an uprising against the conquering forces of the Roman Empire in AD 60 or 61. She personally led battles against the Romans before being defeated and taking her own life.

- In 2000, women comprised just 4% of all US military veterans, but it's estimated they'll be 18% in 2040.

- Marina Raskova was the Red Army's first combat pilot. She was killed during the Battle of Stalingrad in 1943.

- About a quarter of Eritrea's fighters were female during its War of Independence (1961-1991) from Ethiopia. Today, young women are conscripted into the Eritrean military.

- "Axis Sally" was the nickname for two American women—Mildred Gillars and Rita Zucca - who broadcast pro-Axis propaganda during World War II. Both women served time in prison for their Axis activities.

- Ulrike Meinhof was a founding member and the ideological brains behind the 1970s German leftist terrorist group, Red Army Faction/Baader Meinhof Group. She died in prison in 1976.

- In 2005, American soldier Leigh Ann Hester (deployed to Iraq) became the first female since World War II to be awarded the Silver Star and the first ever to be cited for valor in close quarters combat.

- In 1976 the US service academies began admitting women and in 1980 the first 54 graduates entered the military as officers.

- In the conservative Islamic nation of Iran, women serve in the Basij volunteer militia. It's estimated that there are 600,000 women combat capable in this force.

- Although the overall number of enlisted people in the US military decreased by 738,000 from 1973 to 2010, the number of active-duty enlisted women grew from about 42,000 to 167,000.

- Before Gal Gadot was an actress and model, she served two years in the Israeli Defense Forces (IDF). She said her IDF experience helped with her film roles.

- The Women's Army Service Pilots or WASPs was established by the US Army in World War II. The WASPs primarily ferried combat planes between bases, which allowed more men to fly combat missions.

LEECHES, ALLIGATOR DUNG,
AND TAPEWORMS

○ Ancient Egyptian contraception prescriptions included injecting a mixture of "excrement of crocodile mixed with sour milk" into the vagina. I'm sure it worked, just not in the way intended!

○ If you're desperate to lose weight, you can buy a pill that contains a tapeworm egg. Experts warn that although these pills may contain tapeworms, and you may lose weight, the risks far outweigh any benefits.

○ The idea of magnetic therapy is that magnetic fields in the human body can be manipulated to prevent or cure illnesses. Believers often wear magnetic rings or necklaces.

○ The Marche des Feticheurs in Lome, Togo (aka The Akodessawa Fetish Market) is the world's largest voodoo market. You can buy everything needed for traditional medicine there, including crocodile skin and monkey heads.

○ Milkweed has a long history of medicinal use throughout the world. It's been used to treat lesions and warts, but it can also be toxic.

○ Traditional Chinese medicine holds that bear testicles are an aphrodisiac, and the dried seahorse is supposed to help erectile dysfunction as well as asthma, arthritis, and incontinence.

○ The powder of ground-up mummies was a medical prescription in Europe and the Middle East in the Middle Ages. I guess that's why mummies are so rare today!

○ A fecal microbiota transplant (FMT) is literally transferring the poop of a healthy person to a sick person. It's used to treat *clostridioides difficile* infection.

○ "Trepanning" is the term for boring a hole in a person's head to relieve pressure or alleviate some perceived disease or ailment. The earliest known trepanning was done around 6,500 BCE in France.

- "Bloodletting" was a common medical treatment from ancient times through the 19th century. It involved cutting, piercing, or using leeches (see below) to ensure "equilibrium" of the body's fluids.

- The 16th-century Chinese physician, Li Shizhen, was certainly a genius, but his prescription for an abdominal mass on a child is questionable: "boil rat meat until it is mushy and eat it like having porridge."

- India is the site of the earliest dentistry. The people of the Indus Valley Civilization in India (3,200-1,900 BCE) practiced dentistry and the earliest tooth drilling took place even earlier in India, around 7,000 BCE.

- Bee venom therapy is simply allowing yourself to be stung by one or several bees. The painful practice has been used to treat arthritis and multiple sclerosis.

- It's estimated that populations in some countries in Asia and Africa rely on traditional medicine for 80% of their healthcare. This has led some countries to include traditional medicine in medical school curricula.

- The first doctor to use anesthesia in China, and probably the world was Hua Tuo (AD 140-208). The medicine was made from wine and cannabis.

- During the 1800s, traveling merchants often sold "miracle tonics" known as "snake oil." Snake oil was usually nothing more than mineral oil with some common additives.

- Hirudotherapy is the medical practice whereby leeches are applied to a person's body to reduce swelling in the tissue. The leeches also release an anticoagulant called hirudin into the blood. The FDA actually approved this therapy in 2004.

- The ancient Indian physician, Sushruta, wrote the Sanskrit medical text known as the *Sushruta Samhita* in the 6th century BCE. The book identifies illnesses and treatments for them.

- Another seemingly strange treatment the FDA approved in 2004 was maggot debridement therapy (MDT). It turns out that maggots work better than some treatments for cleaning wounds!

- "Cupping" is a practice where a specialist heats a cup or cups, and then presses them on the skin of the patient to "draw out" diseases.

- The ancient Babylonian scholar, Esagil-kin-apli, wrote a medical text known as *The Diagnostic Handbook* between 1,067 and 1,046 BCE. The text is an interesting blend of science and magic.

- In 1979, writer Norman Cousins claimed to have cured collagen disease through a regimen of laughter. It's no laughing matter that he was cured.

- Insulin coma/shock therapy was a treatment where patients would be given an overdose of insulin, putting them into a temporary coma. It was often used to treat schizophrenia.

- The Aztecs were warrior people who developed medicines that suited them. They knew how to set the broken bones of their warriors and sutured instead of cauterizing wounds.

- In South Africa, six out of eight medical schools teach elements of traditional and alternative medicine alongside the standard med school curriculum.

ALL ABOUT ENERGY

○ Natural gas is the leading source of electrical power in the US. In 2021, natural gas was the source of about 38% of the country's power and was the top source in 19 states.

○ Modern "windmills" are so much more complex than they were in the days of Don Quixote. Wind turbines can be 300 feet tall and have as many as 3,000 parts.

○ "Biomass" refers to any plant-based material that can be used as fuel. This can include wood for fires, wood pellets, biofuels, and even animal and human poo (remember methane?).

○ When NASA launched the Vanguard 1 satellite on March 17, 1958, it was the first satellite to use solar electric power. It's still orbiting the Earth!

○ Oil accounts for about 39% of energy consumption in the world. Many developing countries use oil as a source of electrical power and industrial nations use it for their vehicles.

○ Biofuels are fuels produced from plant-based materials. Ethanol is biofuel commonly made from sugarcane or corn to produce fuel for automobiles. It's often mixed with standard gasoline.

○ Coal has dramatically declined as a source of electricity in the US since the early 2000s. Still, in 2019, it was the source of about 19% of power in the US.

○ Renewable energy refers to any energy source that can be naturally replenished. Solar, wind, hydro, and biofuel are all forms of renewable energy.

○ The largest power outage, or "blackout", in history was the 2012 Indian blackouts that affected 620 million people on July 30-31, 2012. India also holds the second spot for its 2001 blackout.

○ Although green initiatives have increased the use of solar power, it still only accounts for .003% of global energy consumption.

- The first car that could run entirely on ethanol was the Fiat 147, sold in Brazil in 1978. Brazil has since led the world in the production of biofuels.

- Steam-powered engines spread across Europe after Englishman Thomas Newcomen invented the first fuel-burning engine in 1712 and Scottish scientist James Watt invented the Watt steam engine in 1776.

- There are arguments over what's the least efficient source of power - either coal or solar. But no one denies that nuclear is the most efficient source of power.

- Air conditioning units account for the most electricity in American homes. It's followed closely by heating, space and water, and lights.

- Nuclear power is by far the largest source of electricity in France, at over 70%. The US still produces more nuclear power, although it's third in overall American electricity production at 19%.

- "Cold fusion" is the process of doing a nuclear reaction at room temperature. Although only theoretical, cold fusion could potentially be the cheapest and most efficient form of energy on the planet.

- In 2020, renewable energy sources combined for 12% of all US energy consumption. Biomass combined for 39% of that total.

- PetroChina is the largest producer of oil and gas in Asia. The US-based energy company, Exxon, is the top energy company in the world in market capitalization.

- No US state uses wind as its primary source of electrical power. But it's the second source of power for Iowa, Kansas, South Dakota, North Dakota, and Kansas.

- The US consumes more than a quarter of the oil consumed in the world but less than 1% of that is used to produce electricity.

- It takes about 10.4 million BTUs (British thermal units) to manufacture recycled material versus 23.3 BTUs to make them from scratch. The processing of a ton of recycled material takes another 900,000 BTUs.

- Hawaii is the only US state that derives most of its electricity from oil. This is largely due to geography, as getting other forms of energy there is expensive.

- In 1825, the US still got nearly 100% of its energy from wood. As the country entered the Industrial Revolution that changed, so that in 1850 coal was the source for about 10% of all energy.

- Nuclear energy is the third source of electrical power overall in the US, at about 20%. It's the main source of power in the states of New Hampshire, South Carolina, and Illinois.

- Russia has the largest reserves of natural gas on the planet and the second most coal reserves. Like the US, 20% of Russia's electricity comes from nuclear power.

INTERESTING NATIONAL
FLAG AND ANTHEM FACTS

○ Liberia's national flag is almost a carbon copy of the US with only one star instead of 50. The similarity is that Liberia was founded in 1847 by former American slaves.

○ Saint Helena is a small Caribbean Island that's still a British colony. Still, they wanted a national anthem, so they hired an American named Dave Mitchel, who had never been to the island, to write the tune for them in 1975.

○ Nepal is the only country with a non-quadrilateral national flag. It's the shape of two pennants, one on top of the other.

○ The recognizable "Union Jack" flag of the United Kingdom is a combination of the flags of England, Scotland and Northern Island. The Union Jack is Britain's *de facto* national flag.

○ Most of the sub-Saharan African countries use a combination of yellow, green, red, and black in their flags. It's believed that this is due to Ethiopia being a model for newly independent African nations.

○ The Greek national anthem, "Hymn to Freedom," is the longest national anthem in the length of text. It's a 158-stanza text based on an 1823 poem written by Dionysios Solomos.

○ The "Nordic Flag" is the term used to describe the similar-looking flags of Norway, Iceland, Sweden, Denmark, and Finland. The flag features a cross shifted toward the hoist (left).

○ The lyrics for the "Star Spangled Banner" were written in 1814 by Francis Scott Key, but the song didn't become the US's official national anthem until 1931.

○ National flags evolved from military flags, which have existed for centuries. The Dutch flag and the British Union Jack emerged in the 1600s as the first true national flags.

○ National anthems became common in Europe during the rise of nationalism in the 1800s. The "marching style" of many national anthems is also indicative of that era.

○ The tiny European nation of Andorra's national anthem, "The Great Charlemagne," is narrated from a first-person perspective. It's the only national anthem to do so.

○ Green is a popular color in the flags of many Islamic countries. Green was the color of the Fatimid Dynasty and is the color of Paradise in the Quran.

○ Canada didn't have an official national flag until it adopted the "Maple Leaf" flag on February 15, 1965. Before that the Canadian Red Ensign flag was the unofficial flag.

○ Brazil's unique national flag features a globe with 27 stars, representing the nation's 26 states and the federal district. The position of the globe reflects the sky over Rio de Janeiro.

- The oldest national anthem is the Netherland's "Wilhelmus van Nassouwe," which dates back to at least 1572. The song didn't become the country's *official* national anthem until 1932.

- Red and gold were the traditional colors of most communist/Marxist states. This color scheme can be seen today in China's national flag.

- Italy's national anthem, "Il Canto degli Italiani," didn't become official until 2017. That may have something to do with the verse being more than a little unflattering toward Austria.

- The national flags of Australia and New Zealand both feature the Southern Cross constellation, but the stars on New Zealand's flag are red. Australia's flag also has the "Commonwealth Star."

- The flags of Switzerland and Vatican City are the only two national flags that are perfect squares. The rest are all rectangles with the exception of Nepal's flag.

- When Czechoslovakia became a country in 1918, the national anthem was half Czech opera and half Slovakian folk song. When the nation split into the Czech Republic and Slovakia in 1993, both groups simply took their half of the song with them.

- Japan's national anthem, "Kimigayo," is the shortest in the world in the length of text. It's also probably the oldest, being based on an ancient Japanese poem.

- From 1977 until 2011, Libya's national flag was just a green field. It was the only national flag at that time that had just one color.

- Purple may be the color of royalty, but it just isn't popular with national flags. The flags of Nicaragua and Dominica are the only two that have purple.

- The national anthems of Spain, Bosnia and Herzegovina, and San Marino are the only ones with no lyrics. I guess you'll just have to hum along!

- Belize has the reputation of being a fun, tropical country. I guess that's reflected in its national flag, which has the most colors of any other flag with 12.

SPACE AND BEYOND

○ Earth is located within the Milky Way galaxy. The Milky Way is about 100,000 to 200,000 light-years in diameter, but it's just one of possibly billions of galaxies in the known universe.

○ The star Alpha Scorpii, or "Antares," is more than 550 light-years from our Sun but it's the 15th brightest star in the sky and has 15 times the mass of the Sun.

○ Although Mercury is the closest planet to the Sun, Venus has the hottest average temperatures at 867 °F.

○ Alpha Centauri is the closest solar system to our own at only four light-years away. It has two stars and a planet that could potentially sustain life.

○ Captured German rocket scientists helped the early American and Soviet space programs. The Soviets, though, had developed rocket technology earlier, giving them an early advantage in the Space Race.

○ NASA started the National Aero-Space Plane (NASP) program in 1986 to build the world's first passenger, suborbital space liner. It was cancelled in 1993 before there were any flights.

○ Mercury and Saturn are both visible to the naked eye. Their names come from the Greeks and Romans, and when modern astronomy was born astronomers decided to keep the tradition of giving celestial bodies Hellenic names.

○ An astronomical unit (AU) is the distance of the Earth to the Sun. One AU is about 93 million miles or eight light minutes.

○ Priests doubled as scientists in ancient societies. After 1,800 BCE, Babylonian priests/astronomers were the first to document patterns in the movements of celestial bodies by using math.

○ Ceres is the largest asteroid in the solar system as well as a "dwarf planet." The planet/asteroid is also a happening place in the sci-fi TV series, *The Expanse.*

- The terms "astronomy" and "astrophysics" mean the same thing. They both refer to the study of celestial objects and phenomena that take place beyond the Earth's atmosphere.

- El Caracol is a spiral staircase structure located in the Maya city of Chichen Itza that was believed to have been built around CE 906. It's believed that the structure served as an astronomical observatory.

- The planets Mercury and Venus have no moons due to the Sun's gravity. By comparison, the outer planet Saturn has at least 83 moons.

- Most sci-fi TV shows and films depict space battles with raging explosions and fire everywhere. Since there's very little oxygen in space, though, there'd also be very little fire.

- Elon Musk's Space X company was founded in 2002, two years after Jeff Bezos founded Blue Origin. Space X currently focuses on transporting people and materials to the International Space Station.

- The Kuiper Belt is a ring of asteroids, comets, and dwarf planets just beyond Neptune. It's about 30 to 50 astronomical units from the Sun and is about 20 times as wide and as much as 200 times more massive than *the* asteroid belt.

- Jupiter may be comprised primarily of gas, but it still has two and a half times more mass than all the other planets in the solar system combined.

- Richard Branson founded Virgin Galactic in 2004 with the intent of it being the world's first passenger, suborbital space liner. In 2018, the first Virgin Galactic plane made it into space.

- NASA built five space shuttles—*Columbia*, *Challenger*, *Discovery*, *Enterprise*, and *Endeavor* - for the Space Shuttle program (1981-2011). The *Challenger* and the *Columbia* were both destroyed during missions.

- Uranus is visible to the naked eye, but it's so far off that for centuries it was believed to be a star. German astronomer William Herschel proved it was a planet in 1781.

- Galaxies are classified by their shape: elliptical, spiral, or irregular. The Milky Way - our galaxy, not the candy bar! - is a spiral galaxy.

- Writer Gene Roddenberry, who is best remembered as the father of the *Star Trek* world/franchise, had no formal background in astronomy. He was a fan of 1950s sci-fi, though.

○ The Oort Cloud is the hypothesized expanse between the Kuiper Belt and the end of the solar system. The Oort Cloud could be as wide as 2,000 to 200,000 AU and is probably comprised mainly of planetary debris.

○ The *Buran* was the Soviet Union's space shuttle, although it only conducted one unmanned mission before the program was shut down.

○ NASA launched the *Voyager 1* space probe on September 5, 1977. It's now 155.8 AU from Earth but still communicating with Earth. Not bad for '70s tech!

WUNDERKINDER

○ Austrian composer Wolfgang Amadeus Mozart (1756-1791) began composing at the age of four or five. Many attribute the term "wunderkind" to Mozart.

○ The German term "wunderkind" translates literally into English as "wonder child." The term has come to mean "child genius" or child prodigy" in many languages.

○ The origins of child prodigies usually come down to the "nature versus nurture"/genetics or environment argument. Recent studies suggest a combination contributes to success.

○ Many professional athletes were prodigies in their sports as children. Hockey Hall of Famer, Wayne Gretzky, scored 378 goals and 139 assists when he was ten against kids much older than him.

○ Edmund Thomas Clint was an artistic Indian child prodigy who tragically died at the age of six in 1983. He produced more than 25,000 drawings and paintings in his short life.

○ Mental calculators are people who can add, subtract, multiply, and divide large and complex numbers in their heads. Many mental calculators begin as children.

○ The fictional school of Hogwarts in the *Harry Potter* franchise is host to several magically inclined wunderkinder. Only children with magical skills are admitted!

○ Michael Kevin Kearney is a child genius who turned his smart into bucks. After graduating from high school in 1990 at the age of six, Kearney went to college and later made money on trivia game shows.

○ Mozart's older sister Maria was also a musical prodigy, but it was a man's world at the time, so she was pushed into marriage.

○ Perhaps the most infamous of all child prodigies is Ted Kaczynski, better known as the Unabomber. Before his bombing campaign, Kaczynski enrolled at Harvard at the age of 16.

- The late Bobby Fischer became the youngest (at the time), chess grandmaster, at the age of 15 in 1958. Not bad for a high school dropout!

- *Savant* is the French word for a scholar, scientist, or even a genius. In English, the word is more commonly associated with the condition, savant syndrome.

- A 2014 study of 18 child geniuses found that they all had excellent memories. The kids were also sticklers for details.

- If you really like bacon, then there's a good chance you've used the "Makin Bacon" plate. Abbey Fleck was only six when she invented the convenient device.

- Adragon De Mello graduated from UC, Santa Cruz in 1988 at the age of 11. He then decided to be a normal kid and enroll in a local junior high before going to the Florida Institute of Technology.

- The spelling bee is believed to have originated in the US during the 1800s in elementary schools. The Scripps National Spelling bee began in 1941.

- The advanced placement (AP) program opened across the US in 1955. The non-profit organization, the College Board, started the program to offer college-level tests and courses to high school kids.

- Michael W. O'Boyle led a research team in 2005 on computational prodigies. They determined that mental calculations have increased blood flow to their brains when they're computing.

- Montessori schools, or Montessori education, refer to children's curricula that eschew standard, regimented curricula in favor of more freedom. Tests and grades are often discouraged.

- In 1995, 11-year-old Richie Stachowski invented the "water talkie," which is a walkie talkie that can be used underwater. The invention earned him the 1999 Entrepreneur of the Year award.

- Kathleen Holtz passed the California bar exam in 2007, which is a major accomplishment at any age, but it was even bigger since she was the youngest ever at 18.

- The opposite of a wunderkind is a "late bloomer." Some notable late bloomers include Thomas Edison and Albert Einstein.

- Sho Yano is a real-life Doogie Howser. In 2009, Yano became the youngest person to earn an MD from the University of Chicago at the age of 21.

○ Balamurali Krishna "Bala" Ambati holds the *Guinness World Record* as the youngest doctor at the age of 17. Ambati earned his MD from Harvard in 1995.

○ Child prodigies are a popular motif in Japanese anime. The series *Naruto* features several young prodigies, including the protagonist, Naruto Uzumaki.

EAGLE EYES

○ Like mammals, birds are warm-blooded, but they differ in many ways. Birds have feathers instead of fur and lay eggs instead of giving birth to fully formed offspring.

○ Birds are popular pets, with more than 16 million Americans owning at least one. Parakeets, which include about 115 species, are usually the most popular.

○ "Raptor" is the term used for birds of prey such as eagles, hawks, falcons, condors, vultures, and owls. Raptors have strong talons and beaks and excellent vision, which is where the term "eagle eyes" comes from.

○ Albatrosses are adapted to glide more than fly. Because of this, most albatross species aren't found in the equatorial regions where there's a lack of wind.

○ The famous cartoon character, the Roadrunner, looks more like an ostrich than a true roadrunner. Roadrunners typically measure only about two feet from head to tail.

○ Penguins are perhaps the best-known flightless birds, but there are 60 species of birds that don't fly. The largest groups are the ratite, which includes ostriches, emus, and kiwis.

○ Poultry refers to domestic birds kept for their meat and eggs. According to the USDA, poultry is the second most-consumed meat in the world at 33%.

○ A crew of crows is a "murder," a group of owls is a "parliament," a bunch of doves is a "duke," a gathering of peacocks is an "ostentation."

○ The smallest bird in the world is the bee hummingbird at less than an ounce and 2.2 inches long. The largest bird is the ostrich, weighing as much as 340 pounds and sometimes more than nine feet in height.

○ The passenger pigeon was hunted to extinction in North America. The last passenger pigeon was a female named Martha, which died September 1, 1914, at the Cincinnati Zoo.

○ The ancient Greeks associated owls with wisdom and bravery. The owl was one of the goddess Athena's symbols.

○ In the 1963 horror film, *The Birds*, the residents of a small northern California town are suddenly attacked by different species of birds. A combination of real and mechanical birds was used.

○ Storks are the quietest of birds. The syrinxes (the vocal organ of birds) of storks are "variable degenerate," leaving them with the ability to make only minimal vocal sounds.

○ In terms of evolution, birds are directly descended from theropod dinosaurs. Modern birds' closest living ancestors are members of the crocodilian order.

○ The phoenix was a mythological bird that was associated with the Sun-God in Heliopolis, Egypt. The myths vary, but most held that the phoenix would die and be reborn from its ashes.

○ The archaeopteryx is a genus of birds, or bird-like dinosaurs, that lived about 150 million years ago. Some scientists believe they represent the first true birds.

○ Flamingos are known for their distinct pink color and the warm climates they inhabit. But flamingos are also known for their unique courtship rituals and usually mating for life.

○ *Corvus*, better known as crows, are often ranked among the most intelligent animals. Crows communicate with each other, can make tools, and can recognize individual human faces.

○ The Andean condor is the largest flying bird in the world, with wingspans as wide as 10 feet and weighing more than 30 pounds.

○ The Fenghuang was a mythical Chinese bird that had some similarities to the Egyptian Phoenix. The Fenghuang, though, is more of a symbol of stability and the idea of yin and yang.

○ In the summer of 1961, the town of Capitola, California was attacked by a flock of sooty shearwater birds. Although no human fatalities were recorded, it served as partial inspiration for the 1963 film, *The Birds*.

○ Sexual dimorphism is common in birds. In many species, such as the pheasant, males are larger and more colorful, although female raptors tend to be larger than males.

○ Parrots are another family of especially bright birds. Some African grey parrots have been tested at the intelligence level of a six-year-old human!

○ You may be surprised to learn that several birds are considered "toxic," emitting a poison for predators that try to eat them. The pitohui and ifrita birds of Papua New Guinea are toxic, as are some other species.

○ The cartoon character, Woody Woodpecker, is probably the most recognizable red-headed woodpecker in the world. Or is he a pileated woodpecker? He has features of both species.

AMAZING ARCHITECTURE

○ Medieval European castles were improvements on ancient forts and palaces. The European castle-building era took place from about 1000 to the end of the 13th century. Gunpowder and cannons put an end to the dominance of castles.

○ *Feng shui* is the Chinese concept that attempts to harmonize people with their surroundings. In China, it has played an important role in the design of buildings and structures.

○ Architecture refers to the planning, design, and construction of buildings. The open-ended definition can include anything from Gothic cathedrals to public toilets: if it requires planning to build, then it's architecture!

○ The Danyang–Kunshan Grand Bridge in China is currently listed as the longest bridge in the world. The rail viaduct is an amazing 102.4 miles long!

○ The Summer Olympics awarded medals for art from 1912 to 1948. Along with literature, music, painting, and sculpture, medals were awarded for architecture.

○ The Aqua Appia was the first aqueduct the Romans built in 312 BCE. The aqueduct brought about 2,600,000 cubic feet of water daily into Rome from 10.2 miles away.

○ Igloos are traditional snow huts built by the Inuit people in parts of Greenland and Nunavut. The largest igloos had five rooms and could house up to 20 people.

○ Instead of using mortar to hold the brick walls of the buildings in place, Inca architects in the city of Machu Pichu in the 1400s used different techniques. They fitted bricks by using their shapes, doors were usually trapezoidal, and walls were connected with "L" shaped blocks.

○ The barrel vault was first developed by the ancient Egyptians and Mesopotamians, but the Romans used it much more extensively, which inspired later vault designs in Europe.

○ Construction of the Great Wall of China began under Emperor Qin Shi Huang (ca. 221-210 BCE). Most of what we see today, though, was built during the Ming Dynasty (1368-1644).

- Cincinnati, Ohio has a little more than two miles of unused subway tunnels under its streets. Construction began in the early 1900s but permanently ended during World War I.

- The iconic Sydney Opera House was designed by a Danish architect Jørn Oberg Utzon. He won a 1955 competition among 233 entries from 28 countries.

- American Frank Lloyd Wright (1867-1959) designed more than 1,000 buildings and was the father of the "Prairie School" of architecture in the late 1880s and early 1900s. The style is known for its flat lines that evoke the prairie.

- Stilt houses are common in regions prone to flooding and cyclones, but on the Indonesian island of Komodo, they also protect the locals from the Komodo dragon!

- Ferdinand Cheval (1836-1924) was a French mailman who spent his spare time building his ideal home, the "Ideal Palace." It took him 33 years to build the masterpiece, but it still stands.

- Third American President Thomas Jefferson was a true polymath. He knew several languages, excelled in business, was a scientist and designed his Monticello plantation in Virginia.

- American TV "super parent" characters, Elyse Keaton on *Family Ties*, and Mike Brady on *The Brady Bunch*, both worked as architects.

- The skyscraper at 33 Thomas Street in Manhattan looks more like something you would've found in the Soviet Union than in the US. The 550-foot-tall building is notable for not having any windows!

- The Colosseum of Rome, which was completed in CE 80, could house 50,000 spectators. There were 76 entrances and 160 passages and adjustable canvas awnings.

- The world's tallest minaret is part of the Quwat al-Islam Mosque in Delhi, India. Work on the 228-foot-high sandstone minaret started in the early 1200s.

- The statues on Easter Island, known as *moai*, were made from locally quarried volcanic tufa from about CE 1200 to 1500. The island was deforested to make the statues, partially leading to the society's decline.

- "Brutalism" is an architectural style that started in the UK after World War II. It emphasizes utility and minimalism, making it popular in communist countries during the Cold War.

○ The world's tallest building currently is the Burj Khalifa in Dubai, United Arab Emirates. Built in 2010, the building towers 2,717 feet in the air and has 163 floors.

○ Britain Kieran O'Donnell designed the iKozie micro-home to combat homelessness. The homes are portable and measure only 186 square feet.

○ Frank Lloyd Wright's son, John, was also an architect but he's best known as a toy inventor. Wright created Lincoln Logs, which first hit stores in 1918.

SPORTS, THEN AND NOW

○ Football's rules were first codified in England in 1863 by the Football Association of England. It was shortened by many to "socc" and an "er" was added to refer to those who play the game.

○ Dragon boat racing was a popular sport in China 2,000 years ago. It involved teams paddling crew-style boats that were decorated with dragon heads. Today Dragon boat racing is carried out all over the world as a hobby sport.

○ In the Canadian Football League, if the kicking team kicks or punts the ball into the end zone and the receiving team doesn't return it, the kicking team gets a "rogue," which is worth one point.

○ American Thomas Hicks won the gold medal in the marathon at the 1904 Summer Olympics after taking brandy and strychnine. Apparently rat poison acts as stimulant!

○ A vase from Hagia Triada, Crete, dated to about 1,550 BCE, depicts two men wrestling. The vase is important because it's one of the first classical depictions of wrestling.

○ If an Australian Rules Football team has too many players on the field, they lose all the points they've scored until that point of time in the match.

○ *Hastilude* was the term used in medieval Europe to refer to combat sports such as jousting. These athletic events were held in tournaments in celebration of royal weddings or other major events.

○ Sepak Takraw is a unique sport that combines elements of volleyball and soccer, with players using their heads and legs to hit the ball over the net. The current version of the popular Asian game originated in Malaysia in the 1940s.

○ Highland Games are held around the world to celebrate Scottish culture and Scottish sports. The caber toss, stone put, and hammer throw are the most popular events.

- In the International Federation of Football (FIFA) rules, the goalkeeper is the only player on the field who can touch the ball with his/her hands and can only do so for six seconds.

- When the Major League Baseball (MLB) teams - the New York Giants and Brooklyn Dodgers left for California in 1957, the Big Apple was without a National League team until 1962.

- Basketball is now the second most popular sport in the world, with more than one billion followers. Basketball generates over $4.75 billion in revenue in dozens of global leagues.

- Archaeologists have uncovered more than 6,000 ball courts in Mexico alone that the Maya and other pre-Columbian peoples of Mesoamerica used to play the "Ball Game."

- "Zorbing" is a "sport" that involves rolling downhill inside a plastic orb that looks like a hamster ball. It started in New Zealand in 1994.

- Soccer/Football is like a religion in Brazil, which is probably due in part to the country winning FIFA World Cups: in 1958, 1962, 1970, 1994, and 2002.

- Shin-kicking is a combat sport that began in England in the 1600s. It's performed just as the name indicates, which makes it no wonder why the "sport" has remained in England.

- When ancient Egyptian kings reached their 30-year jubilee, they would do a ritual run around the mortuary complex. The age of the king didn't matter, so luckily, they weren't timed!

- The tallest listed National Basketball Association (NBA) player in history was Romanian Gheorghe Mureșan, who was listed at 7'7. He may have had an inch on Sudan born NBA player, Manute Bol.

- The sport of auto racing began with the first cars in the late 1800s. Henry Ford enjoyed building cars and racing them in his spare time from 1901 to 1913.

- MLB is known for being conservative. One rule that should probably change immediately is that if the pitch gets stuck in the umpire's face mask, all runners on base advance one base.

- The Green Bay Packers defeated the Kansas City Chiefs in Super Bowl I on January 15, 1967, at the Los Angeles Memorial Coliseum in Los Angeles, California, instantly creating a boon for the pizza industry.

○ The Latin word *munera* referred to Roman blood sports such as gladiator contests, while *venationes* were public hunts of exotic animals. Both types of events were often held in the same arenas on the same days.

○ Basketball was born in the US, but Canadian born Jim Naismith is its father. Naismith invented basketball in 1891 in Springfield, Massachusetts as an indoor winter activity.

○ Underwater hockey, often known by its more colorful name, "octopush," is another unorthodox sport to come out of England. It was started in 1954 in Southsea.

○ The most popular ancient Minoan sport was bull-leaping, although the rules and why the game was played remain a mystery because the Minoan language hasn't been deciphered.

HE DIDN'T REALLY SAY THAT, DID HE?

○ Late MLB hall of famer, Yogi Berra, is known for many colorful quotes that often didn't make sense. "I really didn't say everything I said," is one of my favorites "Yogi-isms."

○ A malapropism is the incorrect use of a word in place of a word with a similar sound. Yogi Berra was notorious for malapropisms.

○ "Let them eat cake!" Well, maybe not. There's no evidence that French Queen Marie Antoinette said those words in 1793, although the sentiment was there and was enough for her to lose her head!

○ Everyone knows that Sir Arthur Conan Doyle's iconic character, Sherlock Holmes, said, "Elementary, my dear Watson," right? Wrong! That quote was never made in a Doyle book.

- Fictional character Tony Soprano declared in the last season of the *Sopranos* that he was "prostate with grief" over the death of his nephew.

- A "Freudian slip" refers to a misstatement or "slip of the tongue," where the speaker says something that is often inferred to mean something else, often sexual in nature.

- Another fictional character known for his humorous malapropisms is Ricky from the Canadian comedy *Trailer Park Boys*. Ricky did whatever he could to avoid arrest, including giving the police an alias "mating (maiden) name."

- A "semantic change" is when the meaning of a word changes for a variety of reasons. For example, "factoid" once meant "an inaccurate statement believed to be true" but it now commonly means a minor or trivial fact.

- Do "Nice guys finish last"? Well according to late MLB great, Leo Durocher, they actually finish in seventh. In 1946, Durocher actually said, "The nice guys are all over there, in seventh place."

- George Washington is often quoted as saying "I cannot tell a lie," after getting caught chopping down a cherry tree. The quote and the tree are fictional!

- Malapropisms are common in the political world. Former US president George W. Bush was known for them, but they transcend political affiliation and national borders.

- "Play it again, Sam" was never uttered by Humphrey Bogart in *Casablanca*. The real quote is "Play it, Sam," ("again" is missing) and it was said by Ingrid Bergman.

- The phrase "Don't fire until you see the whites of their eyes" has been attributed to Andrew Jackson at the Battle of New Orleans and various generals at the Battle of Bunker Hill. The true speaker remains a mystery.

- When asked about why she wasn't in a relationship, actress Jennifer Lawrence answered, "I don't feel like there is a hole to be filled."

- A mondegreen is when a misquote takes on a new meaning. Mondegreens are common in music, but they can also be found in other media as well.

- Mayor Richard J. Daley of Chicago was a colorful character whose mouth sometimes got him into trouble. He once referred to the organization Alcoholics Anonymous as "Alcoholics Unanimous."

- The late Russian Prime Minister Viktor Chernomyrdin is best remembered for his many gaffes. One of the best was, "Better than vodka, there is nothing worse."

- "There's a sucker born every minute" is in some ways proven true by how many people believe that circus man P.T. Barnum said it. He didn't!

- This list wouldn't be complete without a Bushism or two. Former President Bush uttered one of my favorites on May 10, 2000: "I think we agree, the past is over."

- American TV actress Heather Locklear mentioned her ex-husband Tommy Lee in a live interview when discussing her bedroom. Her then-husband, Richie Sambora, probably wasn't pleased.

- The late professional wrestler and commentator, Robert James Marella, AKA, Gorilla Monsoon, is famous for saying things that didn't make sense. One of them, "They're literally hanging from the rafters," has become a viral meme.

- A clever internet meme is the "quote," "The problem with quotes on the internet is you never know if they're genuine." Although the statement has some truth, it's usually attributed to people who died long before the internet was invented.

- Founding Father Benjamin Franklin was known to enjoy imbibing on booze occasionally, but he never said, "Beer is proof that God loves us and wants us to be happy."

- Perhaps the best mondegreen is in the rock band Manfred Mann's Earth Band's 1976 hit, "Blinded by the Light." The line in question goes, "revved up like a deuce" but most people think it says, "wrapped up like a douche"!

- Although US President Teddy Roosevelt did say, "Walk softly and carry a big stick," the original source was an African proverb.

REDWOODS, OAKS, AND PALMS

○ A tree is defined as a plant that has a long stem or trunk. So, it's the trunk that separates trees from bushes, flowers, and other plants.

○ There are about three trillion trees on Earth, which comes to about 420 trees per person. Forests cover about 30% of the Earth's surface.

○ The most famous tree in the world is the Bodhi Tree, located in Bodh Gaya, India. Buddhists believe that the Bodhi Tree is the place where Buddha received enlightenment.

○ Trees are spermatophyte or seed-bearing plants. It may seem strange, but trees' sexual organs are visible (phanerogam) - their flowers!

○ Redwood trees are actually members of the Sequoioideae sub-family of the Cupressaceae family. They are the largest and tallest trees in the world.

○ A boreal forest is a pine forest in the northern latitudes that is often known by the Russian term, *taiga*. There are no natural boreal forests in the Southern Hemisphere.

○ Oak trees are members of the beech family. With more than 500 species, oaks are most abundant in North America: Mexico has about 160 species and there are about 90 in the US.

○ Methuselah is the name of a Great Basin bristlecone pine tree in Inyo County, California that's believed to be the oldest in the world at 4,853 years old!

○ More than half of the world's forests are within the borders of Russia, China, the United States, Brazil, and Canada. In contrast, the sovereign states of Vatican City, Monaco, and Nauru have no forests.

○ Hardcore University of Alabama fan, Harvey Updyke, poisoned the oak trees on rival Auburn University's campus in 2013. The "prank" got Updyke six months in jail.

- Size isn't everything. Although trees tend to be bigger than bushes, this isn't always the case. The primary difference is that bushes don't have a single trunk.

- Unfortunately, about 15 billion trees are cut down annually on the planet. Fortunately, at the current rate, it will take about 200 years to cut down every tree on the planet.

- "Forest bathing" is a form of natural mental health therapy where a person simply spends time in forests. The activity is officially sanctioned by the Japanese government, which calls it *shinrin-yoku*.

- A rainforest is defined as a forest that has a continuous canopy, vegetation that's dependent on high levels of moisture, and has epiphytes and lianas. Rain forests can be tropical or temperate.

- According to geology, the Earth is about 4.5 billion years old, but it wasn't until about 385 million years ago that the first true trees evolved.

- You may think of Australia as almost entirely deserts and beaches, but that's only part of the picture. Forests cover about 19% of Australia's land area.

- A single cottonwood tree can release 40 million seeds in one season. The seeds can then float through the air for days, much longer than any other type of seed.

- In Norse/Viking mythology, Yggdrasil was the name of a giant tree of life. Yggdrasil formed the trunk around which the worlds of humans, gods, and giants were based.

- The age of all trees can be determined by looking at their growth rings through a cross-section of their trunks. Removal of the bark can deform the rings.

- Brazil's most famous forest is the Amazon Rainforest, but it isn't the only notable forest in the country. The Atlantic Forest runs along the eastern coast of Brazil, stretching inland into Argentina and Paraguay. The ecoregion encompasses major cities like Rio de Janeiro and Sao Paulo and is home to more than 148 million people.

- Not all members of the Arecaceae, or palm family, are trees. Many palms are actually bushes and vines, but even palms that are considered trees don't have tree rings.

- Laurel forests are known for high humidity but mild temperatures. They are found in areas throughout the southeastern US. Laurel, Mississippi is near the laurel forests.

○ A single, mature tree can absorb more than 48 pounds of carbon dioxide every year and release oxygen back into the air. This is why trees are important in urban areas.

○ Former "tough man" champion, actor, and American icon, Mr. T, angered the residents of his posh Lake Forest, Illinois neighborhood when he personally cut down 100 oak trees. I guess he didn't pity those trees!

○ The term "jungle" generally refers to tropical rainforests, which is strange when one considers the origin of the word. The jungle is Sanskrit word that means "dry" or "arid land."

A PERSON HAS TO WORK

○ When different areas of the world began entering the Neolithic Period after 10,000 BCE, the "division of labor" began. This was when the specialization of certain tasks and "jobs" as we know them began.

○ The "royal cup-bearer" was a prestigious and trustworthy position in pre-modern societies. The cupbearer would pour the king's drinks and taste them for poison if needed.

○ In the Keynesian view of modern economics, low unemployment is more important than low inflation. Government spending is encouraged to keep employment levels high.

○ If you're patient, nimble, and have plenty of endurance, you may want to give being a human statue a try. As the name indicates, you get paid to stand like a statue for as much as $100 an hour.

○ Before he made his name in electricity, Nikola Tesla worked as a ditch digger in 1886 for $2 a day, which wasn't too bad for the time.

○ Mike Rowe became a household name hosting the hit TV show *Dirty Jobs*. He later revealed that the worst job he ever tried was as a Coast Guard buoy tender.

○ Child labor has always existed in some form, but when the Industrial Revolution began in the 1700s things got out of hand. The first laws protecting child workers were passed in England in the 1800s.

○ A soap-boiler is one who makes soap for a living. It's a tough job if you have any type of allergies, but it can pay about $20 an hour.

○ Indentured servants were people who were required to work without pay for a number of years. That status was often, but not always, the result of unpaid debts.

○ Believe it or not, there's plenty of money to be made from collecting animal urine. Coyote urine is sold commercially as a pest repellent.

○ Serfs were agricultural workers in medieval Europe who were bonded to the land. Serfs couldn't be bought and sold and typically had more rights than chattel slaves.

○ "Professional sleeper" is another legitimate occupation. Pro-sleepers can get paid to test mattresses and pillows, take part in medical/scientific research, or even be part of an art exhibition.

○ In pre-modern societies, eunuchs were often able to land some of the best jobs in the royal courts. The problem was you had to be castrated!

○ A person can make up to $1,000 a week being a professional "line stander." You get paid to stand in line for tickets, new phone releases, or other limited release items.

○ The Black Death of 1347-1353 was a major factor in the decline of serfdom in Western Europe and the rise of free(er) labor. Still, serfdom persisted in Russia until 1866.

○ Young Japanese women with good personalities have found a niche as rent-a-girlfriends. These young women simply go on dates with men, but absolutely no hanky-panky is allowed!

○ Nineteenth-century philosopher, Karl Marx, believed that world history could be summarized as a struggle of the "haves" versus "have nots." In Marx's time, it was the proletariat (workers) against the bourgeoisie (upper class).

○ If you've spent time in a major city in the English-speaking world, then you've probably come across squeegee men. They'll wash your car windshield, sometimes after spitting on it!

○ Professional mourners have been hired for funerals since ancient times. You may be surprised that it's still a gig you can get in some places, especially in China.

○ Guilds were formed in medieval Europe as professional organizations of skilled workers and merchants. Guilds provided the framework for both modern business syndicates and labor unions.

○ The Japanese are known for being polite but when it comes to their subways, they're not afraid to push people around. Professional "pushers" (*oshiya*) make sure the trains are packed.

○ If you don't mind snakes, you may want to consider being a "snake milker." It can be a little dangerous, as the job is to "milk" the venom from the snakes, but it pays about $66,350 a year.

○ The Delhi Sultanate was formed in 1206 primarily through the efforts of a class of Turkish slave-generals. Despite their status, these slaves had the best jobs in the sultanate.

○ If you can get past the taboo, and the smell, then check out being a professional dog food taster. Don't laugh, it can pay between $30,000 and $70,000 a year!

○ *Cuida carros* are common in many cities in Latin America. For a few pesos, they'll watch your car while you get something to eat. Believe me, it's worth your money!

THE EARTH IS ONE BIG ROCK

- ○ Geology is the Earth science that studies rocks and their composition and changes that happen but can also include liquids on the planet. The study overlaps with many others.

- ○ Since the Earth is a sphere, depictions of it on flat maps result in the poles being depicted abnormally large. This type of map is called the Mercator projection.

- ○ The Earth's rocks are divided into three categories: igneous, sedentary, and metamorphic. Metamorphic rocks are formed when igneous, sedentary, or older metamorphic rocks are subjected to intense temperatures or pressures.

○ Cartography is the study of maps and the science of creating them. Modern maps can be political, geological, topographical, or meteorologically orientated, just to name a few categories.

○ The Queen Charlotte Fault in Canada and Alaska connects with the Fairweather Fault in Alaska to create an earthquake zone that's more active than the notorious San Andreas Fault. Alaska records more earthquakes than California.

○ The lithosphere is the crust and the upper mantle of the Earth's surface. Geologists divide the lithosphere into oceanic and continental lithospheres.

○ In 1935, Charles Francis Richter presented his "Richter scale" to the scientific community to determine the magnitude of earthquakes. The system has since been revised and renamed the local magnitude scale, but it's based on Richter's work.

○ Igneous rocks are formed from magma cooling in the Earth's crust. They make up about 90-95% of the Earth's crust by volume and about 15% of the land surface.

○ Silicates comprise the majority of the Earth's mantle. The mantle comprises 67% of the Earth's mass, 84% of its volume, and is 1,800 miles thick.

○ The New Madrid seismic zone extends from Missouri's boot-heel north into the southern tip of Illinois and south into northeastern Arkansas for about 150 miles in total length.

○ The earliest maps were actually maps of the land of the afterlife. Coffins in ancient Egypt's Middle Kingdom (ca. 2,055-1,650 BCE) were painted with schematic depictions and the route the deceased would take.

○ The moment magnitude scale is based on the Richter scale, although it's more precise. It was proposed in 1979 by Thomas C. Hanks and Hiroo Kanamori.

○ The geological theory of "plate tectonics" is that the Earth's lithosphere is comprised of several, moving masses known as tectonic plates. The process began about 3.4 billion years ago.

○ The "Hawaii hotspot" doesn't refer to that state's nice weather, but it is a hotspot of volcanic activity. The USGS lists six active volcanos on the islands.

○ Lapis lazuli is a dark blue metamorphic rock that is primarily found in Afghanistan but also in a few other places in the world. It was popular in ancient jewelry.

○ Sedimentary rocks are formed when rocks, minerals, and organic matter accumulate and cement in layers. About 8% of the Earth's crust is a sedimentary rock.

○ The Great Chilean Earthquake of 1960 is the most powerful earthquake ever recorded. The quake measured 9.4-9.6 on the moment magnitude scale. The quake triggered a tsunami and mudslides.

○ *Sapphire & Steel* was a British 1980s sci-fi series about two 'time travelers' played by Joanna Lumley (Sapphire) and David McCallum (Steel). Other characters were also named after minerals.

○ Scientists believe that the next "supercontinent" to form will be the combination of Eurasia and the Americas, which they already call "Amasia." Don't worry, though, this won't happen for about 200 million more years.

○ Basalt is the most common igneous rock on Earth, comprising about 90% of all volcanic rocks. It's also the most common rock on the Earth's crust.

○ The Greek geographer, Ptolemy (ca. CE 100-170), made the first map that showed the Earth as a sphere. He also included longitude and latitude lines and correctly hypothesized there were more continents.

○ Gemstones are mineral crystals that are often cut and made into jewelry. Sapphire, ruby, emerald, and of course, diamond, are all gemstones.

○ In December of 1811 and January of 1812, the New Madrid earthquakes registered what geologists believe was as high as an 8.2 "measure of magnitude." They were the most powerful earthquakes east of the Rockies in recorded history.

○ A *mappa mundi* refers to a medieval European map of the world. These maps were often pie shape diagrams that divided the Earth into zone, thirds, or quarters.

○ Antarctica is actually home to many volcanoes, 138 in West Antarctica alone. Although most of Antarctica's volcanoes are subglacial, there are four active ones on the mainland.

REBELS AND REVOLUTIONARIES

○ Revolutions are often defined as sudden, major changes. Revolutions can be political, social, or even technological and can happen anywhere, although they are most common in the modern era.

○ The "Neolithic Revolution" describes the transition humans made from a hunter and gatherer existence to domestic agriculture and a sedentary existence after 10,000 BCE.

○ Political revolutions in the modern sense were quite rare in the ancient and medieval eras, although coup d'états, assassinations, and palace revolts were common in some cultures.

○ The term *guerilla* is derived from the French or the Spanish word for war, *guerre/guerra*. It began to be used to describe those who engaged in asymmetrical or irregular warfare during the Napoleonic Wars in the early 1800s.

○ A civil war generally involves factions fighting within a country for control, or to separate and form their own countries. Political revolutions generally aim to overthrow the existing political establishment.

○ The American Revolution (1775-1783) is viewed by some historians as more of a civil war than a revolution because the government in London was never threatened with replacement.

○ Mao Zedong came to power after winning the Chinese Civil War in 1949. He then initiated revolutionary political and social changes during the Great Leap Forward of 1958.

○ Thomas Paine was a true revolutionary among the more conservative American Founding Fathers. His 1776 pamphlet, *Common Sense*, called for American colonists to revolt against British rule.

○ The French Revolution (1789-1799) was a true revolution that overthrew France's monarchy and instituted several social changes. The revolution also led to Napoleon coming to power.

- The Industrial Revolution was a technological and social revolution that began in England in the mid-1700s and continued through the 1800s throughout the world. Steam power was the hallmark of this revolution.

- Ernesto "Che" Guevara was a middle-class Argentine who became a full-time communist guerilla. He helped lead the successful Cuban Revolution in 1958 but was less successful later, dying in Bolivia in 1967.

- The Iranian Revolution of 1978-1979 is also often known as the "Islamic Revolution." It differed from most other modern revolutions because it was theologically based.

- The exact time when the Digital Revolution began is open to debate, but many point to the creation of Apple Incorporated in 1976 as the start.

- Simon Bolivar (1783-1830) was South America's George Washington. Bolivar drove the Spanish from northern South America to become the father of the nations of Colombia, Venezuela, Ecuador, Panama, Peru, and Bolivia.

- "Johnny Reb" was the personification of the average Confederate soldier during the American Civil War. It could be both a slur and a term of affection.

- The "Sexual Revolution" often refers to the period in the late 1960s and 1970s when promiscuity, homosexuality, pornography, contraception, and abortion were all legalized or normalized in the West.

- Maximilien Robespierre (1758-1794) was a radical leader of the French Revolution who ruled France from July 27, 1793, to July 28, 1794. He sent many people to the guillotine until he too finally lost his head!

- In 1848 several revolutions swept across Europe that ended absolute monarchy in many countries. These were very middle-class, or as Marx said, "bourgeois revolutions."

- On March 16, 1917, the Russian royal family was overthrown in a revolution. Then on November 7, 1917, the Bolsheviks overthrew the government. Finally, the Bolsheviks won the Russian Civil War on June 16, 1923.

- Texas became an independent country under the leadership of Sam Houston in 1836. The Texan's victory over the Mexican Army at San Jacinto guaranteed their independence.

- Agustin de Iturbide led Mexico in its war of independence against Spain. He marched into Mexico City on September 27, 1821 and established an independent government the next day.

○ Polish dissident Lech Wałęsa led the Solidarity Movement in the 1980s, which influenced non-violent dissent throughout communist East Europe. The dissent eventually led to the overthrow of communism in parts of Eastern Europe.

○ The Russian revolutions are often referred to as the "February Revolution" and the "October Revolution." This is because Russia was still on the Julian Calendar at the time.

○ Pancho Villa (1878-1923) was a leading figure in the Mexican Revolution (1910-1920). He is best known north of the border for his raid on Columbus, New Mexico on March 9, 1916.

○ Mao Zedong was a writer as well as a statesman and revolutionary. One of his most important books was his 1937 book, *On Guerilla Warfare*.

PROOF OF ESP?

○ Extrasensory perception (ESP) refers to senses or "powers" that are not proven, qualified, or quantified by accepted science. These can include - telepathy, psychometry, clairvoyance, and precognition or retrocognition.

○ The earliest recorded scientific inquiries into ESP were conducted by Joseph Banks Rhine (1895-1980) and his wife Louisa at Duke University in 1930. Although nothing was proven, the Rhines helped establish the scientific merits of studying ESP.

○ "Precognition" is the ability to "see" future events, while "retrocognition" is the ability to see the past. Often, retrocognition is tied with claims to know about "past lives."

○ ESP is generally included in the wider subject of "parapsychology." Parapsychology studies also include ghost sightings and other elements of the supernatural.

○ Canadian psychologist, James Alcock, is one of the world's top critics of ESP and parapsychology. He lectures, writes, and conducts his own experiments that debunk ESP claims.

○ "Psychometry" is the apparent ability to "channel" knowledge of people or events by handling an object associated with it or them. Joseph Rodes Buchanan first coined the term in the 1840s.

○ ESP is often generally referred to as the "sixth sense." Researchers of ESP often argue that the sixth sense is inherent in all or most of us, but some are better able to tap into it.

○ American psychic Nancy Myer claims to have consulted on 300 police investigations in the 1980s and to have given useful information in 80% of those. Clearly, the police believed her because they kept calling her.

○ After World War II, Leonid Vasiliev conducted official research on ESP for Joseph Stalin and the Soviet government. Vasiliev claimed that he was successful, although the program was discontinued.

- Although Joseph Rhine and his Parapsychology Laboratory were officially associated with Duke University, its successor organization, the Rhine Research Center, is an independent, nonprofit organization.

- When New Jerseyan Elizabeth Cornish was found raped and beaten to death in her apartment, the police had few leads until they turned to psychic Nancy Weber. Weber told them to look at the upstairs neighbor, John Reece, who later confessed.

- You've probably seen those cards that have a circle, a plus sign, three wavy lines, a square, and a star, right? They're called "Zener cards" after creator Karl Zener, who invented them to determine psychic abilities.

- From 1966 until she died in 2012, Irene Hughes regularly loaned her psychic expertise to the Chicago Police. Hughes primarily worked to locate missing persons.

- Nearly half of adults in the US believe in the existence of ESP to some extent, with many claiming to have experienced it.

- Zener cards work by shuffling a deck of 25 that has five cards of each symbol. The experiment picks a card, looks at it, and the subject guesses the symbol.

- "Psi" was coined by Joseph Rhine in the 1930s as a substitute for the less scientific sounding "psychic." Psi, therefore, relates to any and all aspects of ESP.

- Charles Honorton developed the "ganzfeld experiment" in the 1970s, which is a test where a "sender" telepathically emits images to a "receiver" for them to guess. Its popularity has declined in recent years.

- "Dream telepathy," or the ability to communicate with another person while dreaming, has had some mainstream acceptance. Sigmund Freud wrote about the possibility of it in the 1920s.

- In a 1932 Zener card experiment conducted by Joseph Rhine, divinity student Hubert Pearce scored a 40%, which was far above the 20% that was considered "chance."

- The CIA became involved in ESP experiments in 1978 by working with the Defense Intelligence Agency (DIA) on the Stargate Project. The project was shut down in 1995.

- In 1938, American spiritualist, Edgar Cayce, claimed that Atlantis would be found in "near Bimini" in "'68 or '69." A large structure *was* found in the waters off Bimini in 1968!

○ According to a YouGov poll, 34% of the respondents believe they've had a psychic experience. The difference is split on gender with 40% of women feeling the psi but only 29% of men.

○ Joseph Rhine outlined his and other ESP experiments in his 1934 book, *Extrasensory Perception After Sixty Years*. Rhine argued that he had scientifically proven the existence of ESP.

○ In a 1984 CIA remote viewing experiment, an officer wrote "The Planet Mars: 1 million BC" on a card. The subject then eerily described an advanced society that was dying from an apocalypse.

○ Psychic Rosemarie Kerr lived in Los Angeles in 1987 but only needed to see a picture of Andre Daigle to know where the missing New Orleanian was. The authorities found Daigle's body, caught his killer, and even brought Kerr to Louisiana to testify in their trial!

FROM FELIX THE CAT TO ANIME

○ Animation technology has come a long way. Early animation involved drawing or painting stills being projected with a device known as a "magic lantern."

○ *Manga* is a distinct style of Japanese cartoons that started in the late 1800s. Manga has several genres, but the rendering of the human figures tends to be similar across time, artists, and genres.

○ A cartoon is any drawn or painted illustration. Once a cartoon is given "life" through various technologies, then it becomes an animation.

○ 'Felix the Cat' was created by artists Pat Sullivan and Otto Messmer in 1919. The crazy cat has since appeared in hundreds of films, shorts, and TV shows.

○ For several decades, the most commonly used method for creating animated films or TV shows was by hand-drawing images on celluloid (cel) sheets. The sheets were then laid over a static background.

○ Cel animation could be quite tedious, with 100,000 or more cels being required for a feature film. CGI animation began replacing cel animation in the 1990s.

○ Original Scooby-Do illustrator, Iwao Takamoto, got his start as a teenage internee in a Japanese internment camp during World War II. Before illustrating Scooby-Do, Takamoto worked for Walt Disney.

○ The 2019 remake of *The Lion King* is currently listed as the highest-grossing animated film of all time, with a worldwide gross of $1,657,713,459.

○ Walt Disney built an empire based on Mickey Mouse and Donald Duck, but what about Oswald the Lucky Rabbit? Disney created Oswald, which was a very Felixesque-looking rabbit, in 1927 and was the first of many successful characters for the animator.

○ Rotoscoping is another early method of animation that involves putting images onto glass panels. The equipment used to do this is called a rotoscope, which was invented by Max Fleischer around 1915. Rotoscoping is still occasionally used.

○ The 2019 version of *The Lion King* also takes the top spot for the most expensive animated film ever made, at a whopping $260 billion, tying with the 2010 film, *Tangled*. That's a lot of pencils and erasers!

○ Perhaps the most *influential* animated film of all time is the 1988 Japanese film, *Akira*. *Akira* was based on a dystopian cyber-punk manga series that has since influenced many books, films, and TV shows.

○ The 1995 film *Toy Story* is generally thought to be the first "classic" animated film using CGI. After *Toy Story*, most animated films have used CGI.

○ Before TV or even film, there were comic strips. Comic strips first became popular in American newspapers in the late 1800s and remain a staple in newspapers that still actually do print editions today.

○ Animators William Hanna and Joseph Barbera first started working together at MGM in the 1930s before forming Hanna-Barbera Inc. in 1959. They went on to create *The Flintstones, The Jetsons, Scooby-Do* and many other successful series.

- The *Looney Tunes* animated short film series ran from 1930 to 1969, making characters such as Bugs Bunny, Sylvester, Daffy Duck, and Porky Pig household names. Warner Brothers revived the series on HBO Max in 2020.

- E.C. Segar was ahead of the times when he created the animated character, Popeye, in 1929. Still, Popeye is considered too "alpha" for today so good luck finding him on reruns.

- Artist Matt Furie created the Pepe the Frog character in 2005, but members of the Alt-Right used the frog as an internet meme in the 2010s. Pepe's current status is in limbo!

- According to Iwao Takamoto, he was told by his boss, William Barbera, to make Scooby-Doo a Great Dane, but instead, he decided "to go the opposite" by making him look silly.

- Broadly speaking, "anime" is any type of Japanese animation. Although the style is usually manga-based, it is much broader. In 2016, Japanese anime comprised 60% of the world's animated TV shows.

- If you grew up in the 1970s or '80s in the US, then chances are you watched Filmation cartoons. *Fat Albert and the Cosby Kids* and *He-Man and the Masters of the Universe* were two of the most popular Filmation series.

- You may not know Mel Blanc by name, but you know his voice. Blanc was the voice of Bugs Bunny and other *Looney Tunes* characters during its original run.

- Walter Lantz, the creator Woody Woodpecker, hired his wife Grace to voice the character in 1950. Grace Lantz was the voice of Woody Woodpecker until 1992.

- Today, many American cartons made in 1930 to 1960s have had some of their content heavily edited due to racial stereotypes. "Blackface" was a common gag in the *Tom and Jerry* series.

- The combination of live-action and animation in film began in the 1920s, but the 1988 blockbuster film, *Who Framed Roger Rabbit*, brought it to another level in terms of effects.

TRUE GUITAR HEROES

○ British guitar god Eric Clapton was always cool, too cool for school. He was expelled from the Kingston College of Art for strumming his guitar too much!

○ About 88% of all guitar players are men, but those numbers didn't stop Joan Jett and Lita Ford from becoming 1980s female guitar heroes.

○ Swedish guitarist Yngwie Johan Malmsteen is revered for his neo-classical guitar compositions and his technical abilities. Malmsteen's guitar of choice is a Fender Stratocaster.

○ Led Zeppelin lead guitarist Jimmy Page's riff on the hit "Stairway to Heaven" is considered by many to be the best guitar solo of all time. It's probably the most recognizable.

○ Frank Zappa was certainly a character, but he was also a great guitar player. Zappa created an eclectic sound to make quirky songs like "Jewish Princess" and "Montana" hits.

○ You may remember Jon Langseth Jr. from the '90s as "Kid Johnny Lang." Although media interest in him evaporated when Lang grew up, he still works as a professional guitarist.

○ Jimi Hendrix may not have had the technical abilities of other guitarists, but his contribution was *how* he played. Hendrix's heavy rifts combined with his on-stage antics set the tone for most later rock guitarists.

○ In addition to being known as the "Country Gentleman," Chet Atkins was called "Mr. Guitar." Atkins was a guitar hero but could also strum a mean banjo and ukulele!

○ The late Eddie Van Halen is best remembered as the guitarist for Van Halen and his many mesmerizing solos, but often forgotten in his guitar solo on Michael Jackson's "Beat It."

○ The Who guitarist, Pete Townshend, developed the "windmill" stunt of strumming his guitar during the 1960s. At 76, Townshend is still windmilling!

- Chuck Berry earned the nickname "The Father of Rock and Roll" in the 1950s by bringing some of the first solos to America. He also became known for his one-foot-hop across the stage as he played.

- Guitar hero Randy Rhoads is a major reason why Ozzy Osbourne stayed relevant in the 1980s, with his mastery on hits such as "Crazy Train." Rhoads tragically died in a plane crash on March 19, 1982.

- Kurt Cobain brought the Grunge style to the masses, but he's often criticized as an overrated guitarist. Unfortunately, his body of work was thin.

- Bluesman B.B. King became a guitar legend for his catchy solos and longevity. From 1959 until 2008, King released 40 studio albums, and 14 live albums and had scores of hit singles.

- In 1999, country crooner Garth Brooks adopted the alter ego of Chris Gaines, a guitar-playing rockstar. Yeah, pretty strange, which is likely why Brooks dropped the experiment after one album.

- Ana Vidović is one of the best-known guitar players you've probably never heard of. The Croatian-born musician is one of the top classical guitar players and began her career as a child.

- Darrell Lance Abbott, better known as "Dimebag Darrel," was the legendary guitarist of heavy metal band Pantera and other groups. Abbot was shot and killed by a crazed fan while he was playing a concert in Columbus, Ohio in 2004.

- Guitarist Ted Nugent built a career in the 1970s as a "solo" artist, but the lyrics on Nugent's early albums were performed by Derek St. Holmes.

- According to legends, blues guitar man, Robert Johnson, sold his soul to the Devil somewhere along a crossroads in the Mississippi Delta. Locals claim the crossroads are at the intersection of US highways 61 and 49.

- Carlos Santana has won ten Grammy awards through his unique guitar riffs that blend Latin, jazz, and rock and roll to create an undeniable style. He learned how to play from his father, who was a mariachi musician in Mexico.

- Skwisgaar Skwigelf and Toki Wartooth are the guitarists for the fictional, animated band, Dethklok. The band has two real studio guitarists and several who play live shows.

- Spaniard Andrés Segovia is often regarded as the top classical guitarist of all time. Before he died in 1987 at the age of 93, he established Spain as the center of the classical guitar world through his play and teaching.

○ Stephen (Stevie) Ray Vaughan was another guitar hero who died in a tragic accident. Vaughan was killed in a helicopter crash on August 27, 1990, en route to Chicago.

○ Country legend Vince Gill made a name for himself playing the acoustic and electric guitar as well as singing. Gill parlayed his guitar skills to play bluegrass and rock as well as country.

○ Legendary bluesman Bo Didley had a long career and influenced many of the top acts in rock, but he's probably best remembered for his rectangular, box-shaped guitars.

PLANES, TRAINS, AND AUTOMOBILES

○ James Watt (remember him from earlier?) devised the concept of "horsepower" to measure the power of steam engines. Even after the horse became obsolete, the measurement continued for mechanical engines.

○ Wilbur and Orville Wright made a living building, fixing, and selling bicycles before they soared through the skies of Kitty Hawk, North Carolina on December 17, 1903.

○ If you're in the UK and are told you're on a "ghost train," don't worry, it's probably not haunted. Also known as "Parliamentary trains," they are routes that are too expensive to close, so companies run reduced service.

○ Steam-powered cars, with external combustion engines, were produced in large numbers in the late 1800s and early 1900s. The size of the boiler needed was one of many reasons for their decline.

○ It's estimated that there will be about two billion cars on the planet in 2040. There were only about 500 million around in 1986.

○ A "model train" is a train, and often an accompanying city, which is done to scale. Train modeling is a serious and often expensive hobby and, according to enthusiasts, should never be referred to as "toys."

○ On October 12, 1997, American folk singer John Denver died when the Long-EZ two-seater he was flying crashed off the California coast. Denver's license was suspended at the time.

○ "Controlled-access highways," also known as freeways, carriageways, and expressways, began with the Long Island Motor Parkway in New York in 1908. The first dual freeway was built in 1924 between Milan and Varese, Italy.

○ Richard Trevithick invented the first steam locomotive and took it for a ride near Merthyr Tydfil, Wales in 1804. The first "journey" was just under 10 miles.

- In 2008, the International Civil Aviation Organization mandated that all flight controllers and flight crew members involved in international flights use English.

- According to a 2015 issue of *Popular Mechanics*, you have a 40% chance of surviving a plane crash if you sit in the tail section. I guess it doesn't pay to get off the plane first!

- Many people believe Henry Ford invented the automobile, but it was German Karl Benz who got the first patent for a motor car in 1886. Yes, Daimler-Benz was his creation as well.

- I'm sure I'm not alone in wondering what's the point of the airplane emergency oxygen masks, right? The fact is, they only have 15 minutes of oxygen!

- Thomas the Train was created by British author Wilbert Awdry for his son, Christopher. Wilbert wrote the stories for his son and made a wooden toy train to go with them.

- The US Federal Aid Highway Act of 1956 was the start of the Interstate Highway system. Although the system was originally conceived as a way to move military equipment across the country, it was immediately available for civilian use.

- You may be surprised to learn that the first electric cars were invented in the late 1800s and that by the early 1900s, about one-third of the cars on the road were electrics.

- For Americans, the chance of being killed in a plane crash is about one in 11 million, while for a car crash it's one in 5,000.

- The fastest bullet train in the world is the SCMaglev in Japan. On 21 April 2015, the SCMaglev reached a world record speed of 375 mph.

- The majority of the world, including 165 countries, drives on the right. The 75 countries that drive on the left are primarily former British territories.

- Tesla Motors, Inc. began in 2003. Elon Musk joined the company in 2004, and it received a $465 million loan from the US government in 2009, and the rest is history!

- Aircraft Transport and Travel Limited was the world's first commercial international airline. The British company began in 1916 with flights between London and Paris.

○ You may be surprised that the chance of dying as a passenger on a train is one in 243,756. This means trains are significantly less safe than planes for travel!

○ If you love fictional cars from film and TV, you have to check out the Volo Auto Museum in Volo, Illinois. The Volo has original and replicas of famous cars, including a General Lee from the *Dukes of Hazard*.

○ Other than takeoff and landing, autopilot is used for most of the flights on most modern planes. With the exception of hitting turbulence, computers are just more efficient.

○ European Russia is connected to its Far East regions partially through the network of trains known as the Trans-Siberian Railway. The network covers 5,772 miles from Moscow to Vladivostok.

ARTISTIC INSPIRATION

○ Spanish artist Salvador Dalí's older brother died nine months before he was born. The influence of his death could be seen throughout Dalí's work, most notably in the 1963 painting, *Portrait of My Dead Brother*.

○ The art of most pre-modern societies was inspired by religion or specific rulers. The artists before the Greeks remain overwhelmingly anonymous, making it even harder to guess their inspiration.

○ Pablo Picasso's 1937 painting, *Guernica*, is a cubist interpretation of the destruction of the Basque town of Guernica during the Spanish Civil War.

○ Van Gogh sure didn't do it for the money. The only painting Vincent van Gogh ever sold before he committed suicide in 1890 was *The Red Vineyard Near Arles*.

- It's difficult to say when "art" exactly began, but humans in the Upper Paleolithic Period (38,000-12,000 BCE) began depicting scenes on cave walls, possibly inspired by their next meal.

- Spanish artist, Francisco Goya, was rejected by art school twice. Goya then moved to Italy for several years where he received inspiration and returned to Spain in 1775 to become one of the greatest painters of his time.

- When the Renaissance began in Europe in the late 1300s, the artists of the era were inspired by the artistic styles and the form of the Greeks and Romans.

- Philippe Starck's 'Juicy Salif' is considered by many to be an artistic masterpiece, even if it's just an ordinary citrus reamer. Starck remains mum on how he came up with the idea or the name.

- War served as the inspiration for one of the true photographic masterpieces of history, *Raising the Flag on Iwo Jima*. The 1945 photograph taken by Joe Rosenthal shows the moment six Marines raised the American flag on Mount Suribachi.

- The *La Pedrera* in Barcelona, Spain is a unique building done in the Modernism architectural/art style of the early 1900s. According to some sources, the chimneys gave George Lucas the idea for the stormtroopers in the *Star Wars* franchise.

- French artist Eugène Delacroix's most famous work is *Liberty Leading the People* (1830). The bare-breasted masterpiece was inspired by the July Revolution of 1830, but it later helped to inspire the French Revolution.

- Impressionism was born in France in the late 1800s as a challenge to existing artistic standards. The style favored real scenes over the ideal and brushed colors over rigid lines.

- The late performance artist Chris Burden claimed to find inspiration in modern television and violence. His 1971, *Shoot*, consisted of him being shot in the arm!

- Porcelain vases from the Chinese Ming Dynasty (1368-1644) are worth a pretty penny today, but they're also one of the first examples of art for profit on a massive scale. Many of the vases were exported to Europe at the time.

- Horror movies and the supernatural, in general, have been the source of masterpieces for quite some time. Tracey Snelling has used her love of horror to produce sculptures that often convey a sense of dread.

- American artist Bob Ross reached an international audience with his *The Joy of Painting* TV show from 1981 to 1994. Ross's easygoing style has influenced millions of people to pick up a paintbrush.

- Pop Art is a style that began in the US and UK after World War II that was influenced by images of modern, capitalistic Western culture. Andy Warhol was the best-known Pop artist.

- Late 19th and early 20th century French Impressionist, Paul Cézanne, was quite open about what inspired him, stating that "a work of art that did not begin in emotion is not art."

- Luke Jerram is a British installation artist who creates images of microbes, viruses, and other things we can't see, which is ironic, or not, since Jerram is color blind.

- Life in early 20th century Iowa is what inspired Grant Wood to become a renowned artist. His most famous painting, *American Gothic*, was a portrait of his sister and their dentist, meant to convey the spirit of the Midwest.

- The Casa do Penedo ("Stone House") in rural, northern Portugal is basically a room that was made from four large boulders from 1972 to 1974. Was the architect inspired by *The Flintstones*?

- In late medieval and early modern Europe, some boys were castrated on purpose to give them the singing voice of a soprano. These unfortunate eunuchs (remember?) were called *castrato*.

- Pop artist Roy Lichtenstein was influenced by a combination of sarcasm and parody in his work. His 1962 painting, *Masterpiece*, best summarized these inspirations.

- Religion in general and Christianity specifically was also a major inspiration for Renaissance art. Botticelli, Michelangelo, and Perugino are just three notable Renaissance artists who were patronized by the Church.

- Artivism is a style of art that focuses on sending a political or social message. Artivism is overwhelmingly more leftwing than rightwing and almost always done in urban areas.

SO EASY A CAVEMAN COULD DO IT?

○ The Paleolithic Period refers to the "Old Stone Age" era of human history. It lasted from about 3.3 million years ago to about 15,000 to 20,000 years ago, depending on the region of the planet.

○ There were several species of humans or *homo*. *Homo habilis* was the first member of the *homo* genus to emerge, living from about 2.31 million years ago to 1.65 million years ago.

○ The oldest known fishhooks were discovered in Sakitari Cave in Okinawa, Japan. The hooks are dated to the "Upper Paleolithic Period," from about 22,380 to 22,770 years old.

○ During the Paleolithic era, the planet was crawling with *megafauna* such as sabre-tooth tigers, mammoths, and mastodons, so humans had to be more intelligent and better organized than what's commonly believed.

○ *Homo erectus* is by far the longest-lived member of the *homo* genus. They lived from about two million years ago to 117,000-108,000 years ago. *Homo sapiens* (modern humans), only emerged just over 300,000 years ago.

○ When Paleolithic people weren't killing mammoths, they were relaxing! Some modern scholars have argued Paleolithic people worked fewer hours and were just as well fed as modern people.

○ The Cueva de las Manos in the province of Santa Cruz, Argentina is a bit of a creepy place. It's known for the hundreds of mainly left hands that were stenciled into the walls sometime between 7,300 BCE and CE 700.

○ The oldest known tools were discovered at the site of Lomekwi, Kenya. The primitive tools date to three million years ago, predating the oldest *homo* by 500,000 years.

○ *Homo neaderthalensis* emerged in Europe about 400,000 and lived until about 30,000 years ago. Modern Europeans and Asians have 1% to 4% Neanderthal DNA on average.

- The atlatl is an ancient spear-throwing device that has been invented independently throughout the world at different times. It's believed the first atlatls were developed about 30,000 years ago by *homo sapiens*.

- The earliest *homo* tool-making culture is known as the Oldowan, which existed from 2.6 to 1.7 million years ago in Africa, Asia, and Europe. The Oldowan was replaced by the Acheulean, which lasted from about 1.7 million years to 130,000 years ago.

- Paleolithic people get a bad rap for living in caves, but caves allowed *homo* species to protect themselves from animals and other *homos*, bury their dead and contemplate their life.

- Paleolithic people sewed their clothing, made skin boats, and other things. The oldest known bone needle, discovered in the Denisova Cave in Siberia, Russia, has been determined to be more than 50,000 years old.

- The Mousterian tool complex/culture from about 300,000 to 30,000 years ago, involving Neanderthals and modern humans. The Levallois technique was used in a knapping procedure (flaking procedure) to produce arrowheads and other tools.

- From about 40,000 to 35,000 years ago, Paleolithic people began developing extensive and intricate cave art. The best-known example is the Lascaux Cave in France.

- Men did the hunting and fighting, while women gathered nuts, fruits, and berries during the Paleolithic Period, but there may have been more gender equality than in later eras.

- "Neanderthal" is often used as a pejorative for someone with a low IQ. The truth is that the Neanderthals had larger braincases on average than modern humans.

- The Clovis Culture lasted from about 13,000 to 11,000 years ago in North America. The Clovis is the best known and was the most advanced and widespread of all North American Paleolithic cultures.

- Perhaps the greatest work of art from the Paleolithic Era is the Venus of Willendorf. The 4.4-inch-high statue of a curvy female was sculpted 25,000-30,000 years ago.

- It was once thought that modern humans wiped the Neanderthals out in endemic warfare, but now scholars believe a number of factors contributed. One is that Neanderthal women had longer gestation periods.

- *Homo floresiensis* is named for the island of Floresiensis, Indonesia where all known remains were found. These people, who lived until about 50,000 years ago, were only about 3'6 tall!

- Britain no longer has any large wild animals, but in the Paleolithic Period the island was home to woolly rhinoceroses, cave lions, and mammoths.

- The oldest known musical instruments are several flutes discovered in caves in Germany that are dated 43,000 to 35,000 years ago.

- Red ochre was one of the most common types of paint used in the Paleolithic Era, but yellow ochre, hematite, and coal from a number of sources, including human bones, were used.

- Bruce Bradley of the University of Exeter and Dennis Stanford of the Smithsonian Museum argue that stone age explorers hopped ice floes in the North Atlantic to get from Europe to North America. Their theory is known as the Solutrean hypothesis.

LIVING IN THE CITY

○ Jericho was the site of one of the world's first permanent settlements and it was the earliest known defended settlement. The Walls of Jericho were first built around 9,000 BCE.

○ There were still more people living in rural areas than urban centers in the world until 2007. Today, about 55% of the world's population lives in cities.

○ Although "urban planning" has existed since the first true cities cropped up 5,000 years ago, it's more of a modern science. In addition to determining the layout of streets, urban planners consider sanitation, zoning, transportation, and other issues.

○ Tokyo, Japan currently holds the top spot as the world's largest metropolitan area with about 37.5 million people. The World Economic Forum predicts that Jakarta, Indonesia will take the top spot by 2035.

○ Çatalhöyük in Turkey was another one of the world's first permanent settlements. Some scholars estimate it had a population of about 6,000 people between 6,700 and 5,700 BCE.

○ It should be pointed out that what constitutes "urban" and "rural" varies among nations and organizations. In the US, towns with more than 2,500 people are considered urban while in Japan it's 30,000.

○ A "megalopolis" is an urban region where major metropolitan areas have overlapped each other. Bosnywash (Boston, New York, and Washington) is the best example in the US.

○ With a population of over 300,000, Murmansk, Russia is the largest city in the world north of the Arctic Circle. The North Atlantic Current helps moderate Murmansk's temperatures.

○ A "suburb" is simply a city that is just outside, and often directly bordering, a major urban city. Suburbs are "urban" according to the basic definition.

○ For many metro areas in Europe and North America, the suburbs just outside the city proper are more populated than the city. The creation of freeways, "white flight," and the availability of public transportation are all contributing factors.

○ With a population of 453 and only .19 square miles of area, Vatican City is one of the smallest "cities" in Europe. It's important to note that it's also a sovereign state.

○ The ancient city of Uruk in Mesopotamia is believed to have been the first urban center to reach a population of 50,000 people. This was accomplished around 2,900 BCE.

○ "Ekistics" is the study of human settlements, which utilizes and overlaps with several other academic studies, including geography, anthropology, and cartography. Ekistics scholars also classify the size of permanent settlements (village, town, city, etc.).

○ Rio de Janeiro literally translates into English from Portuguese as "River of January." Although the state has more than 200 rivers, the name was what the region's first Europeans originally called Guanabara Bay.

○ The US Census Bureau defines an urbanized area (UA) as an urban area of more than 50,000 people, while those less than 50,000 are called urban cluster (UC) areas.

○ Ancient Rome was the first city in the world to reach a population of one million. It did this in the early Imperial Period (after 27 BCE).

○ A "15-minute city" is a planned, residential urban neighborhood where residents are within a 15-minute walk or bike ride to get all of their necessities. A variation of this idea is the 20-minute city.

○ In 1950, the world was less populated and far less concentrated in cities, with 746 million people living in urban areas. In 2014, that number had grown to 3.9 billion.

○ In 2010, 80.7% of the US population was living in urban areas, which includes UAs and UCs, but nearly 94% of the US territory of Puerto Rico was urban.

○ The Home Insurance Building in Chicago was built in 1885 with ten floors and later had two added. It's considered the world's first skyscraper, but unfortunately, it was torn down in 1931.

- Delhi and New Delhi are technically two different entities. New Delhi is the national capital district located *within* Delhi.

- Tenochtitlan was the largest city in the Pre-Columbian Americas. It's estimated the population was at least 200,000 and as much as 400,000.

- Punta Arenas, Chile is the most southernmost city in the world with a population over 100,000. It currently has over 127,000 people.

- Damascus, Syria is often given the title of the oldest continuously inhabited city in the world, with settlement beginning in the 2nd millennium BCE, but there are other claims. Nearby Byblos, Lebanon has been inhabited continuously since at least 5,000 BCE.

- Although the majority of the world's population lives in urban areas, those areas cover less than 1% of the Earth's surface. I guess there's room for growth!

CONCLUSION

I hope you enjoyed reading *Interesting Facts for Curious Minds: 1572 Random, But Mind-Blowing Facts About History, Science, Pop Culture, and Everything in Between*, and if you read it cover to cover you deserve a thanks and possibly a prize! I'm sure you feel a bit more edified, entertained, and ready to tell some of your family and friends about some of the new and interesting factoids you learned.

Or should I just call them facts?

As you read through this book, I'm sure you thought of plenty of other facts that could've been added to each chapter, which is the point of this book - to engage you and get you thinking in a fun way!

And speaking of fun, I'd like to say that everyone involved in the creative process has had plenty of fun creating this book. I know that the world seems bleak at times, so if we can help brighten up your day just a bit, then we're more than happy with the outcome.

So now that you have this engaging and fun tool at your fingertips, it's up to you what to do with this "power." I'm sure you'll use it for good, by breaking it out at a party or gathering with friends and family, or maybe you'll loan it to a friend.

Whatever you decide to do, just remember to always keep thinking and questioning, but don't forget to have fun while you do so. Sometimes the most serious facts in life are also the silliest or strangest!

Made in the USA
Thornton, CO
11/16/23 22:01:24

bef85b0d-efc4-4cf9-b4dc-cc88277abcd9R02